BARBARA AND MY BOYS:

Life Stories of Change, Community and Purpose.

By

Michael Oropollo, Jr. and Debra Warner, Psy.D.

Published By

The Summit on Community Resilience, Intervention, Prevention, and Training (SCRIPT)

Barbara and My Boys: Life Stories of Community Change and Purpose.

Copyright 2019 Michael Oropollo Jr. and Debra Warner, Psy.D.
All Rights Reserved.

No part of this book may be reproduced in any form whatsoever, by photography or xerography or by any other means, by broadcast or transmission electronically or otherwise without permission in writing from the publisher or authors, except by a reviewer who may quote brief passages in critical articles or reviews.

SCRIPT
1409 W Vernon Ave, Los Angeles, CA 90062
ISBN 978-0-578-53158-8

Printed in the United States
1st Printing 2019

ATTENTION: ORGANIZATIONS & CORPORATIONS
Bulk quantity discounts for reselling, gifts or fundraising are available. For more information, please contact SCRIPT@consultant.com

Cover Design: Dave Warner
Photos: Scot Obler, A Better LA

Dedication

To all change agents in the world.

Acknowledgments

From Michael Oropollo, Jr.

I joined Dr. Warner on this book in the winter of 2018, on the heels of working with her on her first book, *His History, Her Story*. Dr. Warner and I were actively promoting it. Before we could fully enjoy its success, Dr. Warner wanted to begin the next project. She laid out the research that she had just completed on gang community violence intervention, charting the effects interventionists had on reducing crime in their neighborhoods. She mentioned that she wanted to write a book about their stories. Five of them volunteered to be interviewed. Beyond that details were scarce, but I was elated to work on a new project. I went into my first interview with an author's mindset – that I would be telling stories. That interview lasted nearly three hours. It took me about ten minutes to understand that the depth and breadth of this book was much deeper than merely telling stories. This was about life and death, tragedy and change; it was about humanity.

It challenged me to reflect on my own practices in dealing with the community and the approach with which I educate my students as a teacher in a public school. Public education is the cornerstone of American society and the foundation of our democracy. As educators, we are the pillars that hold the entire system in place, connecting the past to the present, passing along our values to future generations. We are the innovators and transmitters of knowledge, and as such it is our responsibility to understand the nuances of the issues that affect the people living in our communities. As educators, we must be educated ourselves to the realities of the communities that we serve.

We play an active role in violence prevention by inspiring our students and being creative, enthusiastic, knowledgeable and morally sound individuals. Many of our students lack consistency and stability at home. All too often these environments lead many of our kids down the path of gangs and violence. However, we have the opportunity to be the stability that they seek each day – a smiling face greeting them at the door each morning or allowing them to vent their concerns can go a long way. We mediate at the crossroads of society in all its equal beauty and suffering. In this book, you will discover that many of the solutions to community violence lie in the ability of interventionists and community stakeholders to work in a collaborative manner. Educators serve a critical role in this process.

I would like to thank all of the interventionists around the world who do this selfless work that will never appear on the five o'clock news. Specifically, I would like thank Nikko Deloney, Tommie Rivers, Barbara Jett, James Marks, Anthony Porter, and Dr. Aquil Basheer for educating me on the work that they do. I am humbled and grateful for the opportunity to work with people whose contributions to humanity are so tangible.

From Debra Warner, Psy.D.:

This book represents a journey back to 2008 to my initial meeting with these wonderful champions of life. After hearing about, and finally having the privilege of witnessing firsthand, their great impact on the world, I knew I had to find a way to share their story. Since Michael and I began writing this book, I have struggled with how to adequately convey the proper magnitude of the impact that these men and women have had on my experience of life. This book and the stories it relates are focused on Los Angeles because that is where we reside. However, there are community interventionists all over the world that keep our world safe. It is my hope that sharing these stores will result in more light to be shed on these interventionists around the world.

I remember feeling humble on the day we met these five interventionists. They shared their stories and explained how their past cleared a unique path for them to do the work that they do today. They explained that their work represents their environment and that it is shaped by the unique needs their culture faces. They also noted that not all interventionists are the same as each interventionist must fit their unique culture and environment in the world. As they spoke with forthright honesty and sound resolution, I became certain that their work was about one thing – humanity. I felt captivated and grateful to sit in the presence of such wonderful souls.

Throughout our years of working together, I have come to know them as family. Somewhere in that web of time, I began to call them "my boys" and "my ladies" as a way of expressing my affection, of inserting myself into their world, which they have so kindly welcomed me into. It has become a place to which I belong, a place where I feel safe, comforted and protected. Over the course of a decade of working with my boys and my ladies, I have slept well knowing they are out in the world doing their work. And so, we are inextricably connected.

There are only five community interventionists showcased in this book, but they stand for the hundreds, possibly thousands, of unrecognized men and women across the world that do this work. I have had the absolute pleasure of meeting several of them. It is my hope that reading this book will instill in you the same admiration, understanding and affection for them and their work that I carry in my heart.

Table of Contents

Foreword: Laying the Foundation 1

Introduction 9

Chapter 1: History of Gangs 11

Chapter 2: Community-Based Gang Intervention & Outcomes 22

Chapter 3: Anthony "Ant Dog" Porter 31

Chapter 4: Barbara Jett 39

Chapter 5: James "Blue" Marks II 50

Chapter 6: Nikko Deloney 64

Chapter 7: Tommie "Ttop" Rivers 75

Chapter 8: Interviews with Gang Interventionists 85

Chapter 9: Looking to the Future 98

Chapter 10: Summary 106

About the Authors 108

References 112

Foreword: Laying the Foundation

An Interview with Aquil Basheer, D.Litt.

Who you are and what you do?
I am a revolutionary social activist that started this work back in the late 1960s. I was involved with organizations that dealt with social mobilizing. Those organizations brought the context of community ownership through collaborative processes. I come from the gang culture from a time when that culture wasn't about self-destruction or the destruction of others.

I was fortunate that most of the organizations back in the day, including the organizations that I was involved with, were geared towards social justice initiatives and redirection of governmental policies as opposed to the destruction of each other. From the activist root of that time grew this work of community engagement, urban safety, trauma recovery, self-determination and self-reliance.

Currently I hold the titles of urban safety specialist, comprehensive anti-violence expert, and community crisis consultant. Above all else, I am a practitioner, meaning that I provide direct services on the ground, in the community reducing violence, trauma, and crisis, as well as strategic development in helping organizations, cities, and countries build out their infrastructure in relation to public safety. All of this is to serve the goals of community empowerment and community transformation.

The work is international but it started in Los Angeles?
As I became seasoned in this work, it became obvious that the preeminent objective was to create a rational model for community intervention. This objective was preeminent to all others. At the time that this work began,

we were all individuals from our respective communities. The model needed to be viable in order to work to scale in the city of Los Angeles, and I had aspirations of taking it to the national level. I wasn't focused internationally yet. That came later.

The key to taking the work nationally was a replicable model. The process of creating such a model took years of refinement, errors, and surprises. That was all done here in Los Angeles and in and around all areas of the city – Pacoima, Watts, Compton, South Central – in all of the hot spots. Once we felt that we had a viable model, we took it to a national level to test the hypothesis in other environments outside of our comfort zone of California cities. We ran into headaches and mistakes when we went national, but we refined the process as we did in Los Angeles and then scaled it up internationally.

A point that must be stressed is that this model is not a gang-intervention model. We are gang experts bar none, but we understood from our early, formative years that we were going to intervene in the larger context of comprehensive community mobilization, empowerment, and community ownership. Gang intervention is paramount, but it is one peg in the wheel. We knew we had to stop generalized violence first. No form of community mobilization and ownership can move forward if the community is petrified with fear. We concentrate on violence on all levels, from gangs to interpersonal violence, domestic violence, and societal violence. Gang violence is symptomatic of greater problems in a community. It is in your face, and that is why it needs to be dealt with first.

When you are dealing with gangs, you are dealing with symptoms. If you do not get to the root causes, the source, of why those young bangers are doing what they're doing, you are not going to be able to change the direction of those individuals and the community at large. All you will be doing is putting a bandage on a wound that will continue to fester. We do not concentrate on gang violence per se, but rather what caused the individual to embrace it. Furthermore, we examine what caused that individual to stay in that violent mode and continue doing what they do despite the catastrophic consequences to themselves and others.

Having come from the culture, I know that one cannot simply go into the gang environment simply with the hope of changing it and expect anything productive to happen. You need to have credibility. This credibility is what we call LTO – license to operate. Coming out of that culture, out of the movement, and with the history of action that I had in the movement, that is where my license to operate comes from.

Additionally, I have forty-plus years of involvement on the ground. It does not matter what I did in the 1960s and 1970s. If I wasn't doing those things now, I would have no credibility. I would just be another elder from back in the day. The work I have done over four decades has allowed me to facilitate and nurture connections and relationships within these communities – relationships that allow us to go in and build out the local and national model.

What do interventionists do?

Imagine me being a maestro in an orchestra and all these guys and gals play a different instrument in the orchestra. I have to navigate bringing all these individuals together, bringing out their expertise, and putting the components together in the right way to make the song.

At the time that we were putting together this team, the city was beginning to look at the concept of intervention and how it could play a role in the municipal structure. The purpose of bringing together the team that you will read about in the book was intervention, outreach, equitable service, and violence prevention. The primary purpose, however, was hardcore gang intervention, for the simple reason that no one else had been able to create a structure of turning these individuals into unified assets to the community. That is what we have been able to do with the Professional Community Intervention Training Institute by turning them into professional peacekeepers with certifications and providing them structure and protocols as to how to operate. The key to this entire structure was bringing in shotcallers, or gang leaders, because we had to recruit individuals with true credibility in the community. If they could receive our knowledge and go back to their communities, people would listen to them. Our first class in 2007 had sixty-two shotcallers trained as peacekeepers. The class was based off the intervention work I was doing for many years prior with my company Maximum Force Enterprises. The concept was to bring warring neighborhoods from the city together. The shotcallers represented all of the sections of the city, its major gangs, and were diverse in race and ethnicity. It was a true cross section of the gang community in Los Angeles.

For eighteen weeks we trained these individuals to eat, learn, and work with each other. The thought behind the intimacy and duration was that after eighteen weeks, it would be hard for these people to go back to their neighborhoods and shoot each other, like they would have when they arrived on day one. It is an essential refinement process of behavior protocol, self-reflection, and how to deal with people in a constructive manner. It is much deeper than training. It is a true transformation of the individual – a refinement process. When these rival shotcallers return to their community and begin conversing in open dialogue with a mutual respect, the community is inclined to do the same thing. The change begins with the individual and spreads to the community. As we matured, we began to bring into the academy graduate students from surrounding universities, mental health professionals, law enforcement officers, and fire department personnel so they could humanize one another and change prejudices and biases that each group may have had towards one another. It was necessary to certify and professionalize the gang members to show people working in official capacities that there were diverse components to intervention, that it was not just about gangs.

After the institute was running for several years, I met Dr. Warner. She was an advisory board member with one of our first funders, A Better LA. Dr. Warner provided the expertise of The Chicago School of Professional Psychology. We were so impressed with her work and perspective that we held a class of thirty graduate students from her institution and took them through the entire eighteen-week course. In three years we graduated over seventy of her graduate students as PCITI-certified. That allowed her to see the depth of the work and the mindsets of the interventionists who are involved with our organization. Because of that relationship and the process it has undergone, we made the link from practitioners to academics, which had never been done before. Additionally, Dr. Warner brought a psychological and administrative perspective to us. My trainees knew that they were on to something substantial and meaningful, but they could not describe what it was. Dr. Warner explained the specifics of the thinking patterns that they held, how and why those thinking processes changed, and gave them the descriptive syntax to quantify and communicate from their inner selves.

My role in all of this was that of maestro. I have to be simultaneously on the streets, in city hall, and in the ivory towers of academia. I had to have a multi-linguistic approach, being able to communicate in the very different lexicons of these three arenas, and at the same, getting these different people to speak the same language. Throughout the relationship with The Chicago School, much of our work was validated, and I was awarded with a Doctorate of Letters based on the forty years of my intervention work. The school became a part of our larger, collaborative public safety and academic network. I currently work with and teach at several universities including Alliant University and the University of Southern California. The academic and educational is another critical component in bringing the community together along with public safety, mental health, and our training protocols.

What does this work mean to the communities you serve and society as a whole?

The larger cause of the work that we do is to bring adversarial forces to a table and build a process of peace while simultaneously creating a system for that peace to be achieved. Coming together is fruitless if it is not going to build a blueprint of how other people can do the same thing. There are people all over the world who need to be able to use our work as a template to achieve the same ends in their own communities. Replication is a keystone in this entire endeavor so that people like me can be removed from this process, so that a succession plan can be put into place.

A process creates a system, through trial and error and the discovery of successful components working together to serve a purpose or function. A system-driven process is much more durable to the obstacles of human error, personalities, contributions or lack thereof. The process must move forward because I am just a component that drives it, but the system dictates the direction and function. That is what we have been able to do with the school of PCITI. Through the years of conducting our eighteen-week training course, we have failed our way to success by implementing what works and trimming what does not. When we rolled our system out on the larger scale – in the communities that we serve and eventually with other people taking our process and implementing it in their communities – we saw that we had something that worked.

We continued to refine the process and add collaborative partners, providing us with more tools to use.

We deal with traumatized, marginalized individuals. Regardless of how hard their exterior looks, these people have been traumatized and do not have the resiliency of safety nets that allow them to bounce back. This is within the men and women that we train, as well as the people living in the communities that we serve. The narrative goes as follows: you have stress which turns into distress. If the distress is not dealt with, it turns into crisis. Trauma is created at the nexus of distress and crisis. If you do not deal with crisis, what follows is disaster and finally, catastrophe – where people destroy themselves and others in the process. The importance in the work lies in the ability to disrupt that equation through intervention, proactive prevention, outreach, equitable services, and restorative justice tools that are proven and validated. The end goal is to bring that individual, family, or community back to some degree of normality. If we can bring their short-term life back to baseline, then we can begin to work on the long-term goals. If we can succeed with one family then we can duplicate that success with another, and another, until we can stabilize an entire community and that community no longer becomes marginalized because they have taken ownership to redirect themselves. The community becomes empowered to self-determination, deciding its own identity, as opposed to conceding to the narratives of fear, violence, and economic insecurity. One successful community can be a reflective tool for another, and so this thing spreads.

Inclusion of the people that we serve is an absolute essential element. The advice of experts and the perspectives of policymakers are an important component, but by no means the final solution. Without community inclusion, a somewhat simple, although not easy, process can become unnecessarily complicated. This common mistake actually creates distrust in the people in the community that we are trying to serve and becomes counterproductive to the well-meaning goals of all the experts involved. Who is better to navigate the needs of a particular community than the people who live in it? It all begins with relationships and understanding. People have to know that you understand their why – why they are engaging in these self-destructive behaviors. In a smaller sense, we are dealing with the repairing of people, the root cause that allows a person to accept self-destructive thinking and behavior, as opposed to Band-Aids on an entire system. This is a much larger package than dealing with the hostilities of gang violence in one particular community. The eradication of marginalized communities across the globe benefits society by turning them into functional contributors in their given areas. It stops the perpetuation of degrading self-hate and people wanting to destroy each other because of a lack of resources. This is no small picture but we have to start small – one individual, one family, one community at a time – with the perception of building a framework for people to connect and operate.

Introduction

Tony struggles to get out of bed. It's two a.m. and he just got home from assisting the police with a domestic violence incident in a known gang hot spot. Now he has to go to the scene of a drive-by shooting and hopefully aid in making peace in the neighborhood by arranging a treaty between two warring gangs. He gets out of bed, hoping that he can get a few hours of sleep in his car before he has to go to work.

That's a typical night in the life of Tony, one of the bravest people I have had the pleasure to know. He is a community interventionist. For the past eleven years, I have had the gift of interacting with some very unique people. They are ex-gang members from different rival gangs who have now dedicated their lives to keep others from following their same path. Most have served time in prison, been in shootouts and lived on the wrong side of the law. But now, they risk their lives daily to keep our streets safe by interfacing with law enforcement, first responders and gang members. Community interventionists, who are from these zones, know firsthand what can happen when situations involving violence escalate. They know from experience how things are perceived on the street and how they really are. They risk their lives to create safer communities.

This book tells the stories of five interventionists who work the streets of some of Los Angeles' toughest neighborhoods. It articulates who they were and how they got to be who they are now. Each story has similarities and differences but each provides a close-up of a life most of us only see through the lens of Hollywood fantasy. This book is the reality behind that fantasy. It gives credit for the hard, dangerous and usually unsung work each of these individuals do.

This book utilizes data gathered over six months of following interventionist teams to show how their work assisted in instilling safety on the streets with qualitative and quantitative data. Crime reduction is discussed using data gathered, along with narrative examples. The book will show how community intervention reduces street violence and assists with community policing efforts.

Chapter 1

History of Gangs

Christopher D. Raichel, J.D., M.A.

Gangs in the United States have a long-rooted history with the first gang formation occurring prior to the adoption of the Constitution in the 1780s (Howell & Griffiths, 2010). These gangs, however, lacked structure and organization in order to thrive and have not been documented as a true representation of American street gangs. Indeed, the evolution of modernized street gangs occurred in the late 19th century. Street gangs of today have a sense of durability in that they last throughout multiple generations and have a marked collective identity that is unique to each gang (Pyrooz, Decker, & Fleisher, 2011). More so, contemporary gangs have intertwined criminal enterprise and activity within their gang identities.

Although contemporary gangs engage and identify with criminal enterprise, Coughlin and Venkatesh (2003) suggest that these gangs engage in such conduct as a secondary means of operation and functionality. That is to say, gangs are rooted in a sociological context based on members' race and geographical location. Gangs within the contemporary setting follow the traditional foundations of gangs in which territorial protections are established for those within the gang's territory, allowing the gang to operate in a *de facto* community police manner. Furthermore, gangs aid in the establishment of an identity of the individual within that community along racial and ethnic divides. Street gangs primarily operate in today's context along a single racial identity with a hierarchal structure (Pyrooz, Decker, & Fleisher, 2011).

In order to better understand contemporary gangs, one must have a better understanding of the formation of gangs within the United States from the 19th century (Howell & Griffiths, 2010) and the spread of gangs throughout the United States throughout the country's history.

Gang Roots in United States History

Membership in gangs in contemporary society is thought primarily to consist of Black or Latino individuals. This, however, is contrary to the composition of the earliest gangs traced in the United States, which consisted of either White or Black individuals in New York City (Sante, 1991). With the threat of gangs in the United States, and its eventual spread, research heavily focused on the delinquency of gangs and their members prior to the 1920s (McLean, Robinson, & Densley, 2018). From the 1920s to the 1970s, however, gangs were left out of research and the formation of criminal justice policy. This trend changed with the emergence of illicit drugs within the United States and the social policy shifts that worked to end the presence of gangs given that drugs formed their newly found underground enterprise.

Although research on gangs had been generally limited and omitted from criminal justice policy, gangs were able to form and migrate throughout the early 1900s through different waves within different regions in the United States (Howell and Moore, 2010). The United States had three different regions of gang development and expansion: New York City, Chicago, and Los Angeles. Gang expansions were motivated through unique shifts within specific territories with mass migration and expansion of racial identities throughout the country, as well as enactment of policies that drove further expatriation from original communities to others.

As previously described, gangs were formed in the 19th Century as a way to protect the economic and racial interests of specific immigrants, in particular those of Irish and Italian ancestry in New York City (Howell & Moore, 2010). Maintenance of these gangs was primarily rooted in the context of promoting the group's own ethnic identities within economic zones, as well as advancing their own interests and protecting the territories in which these immigrants lived. With time, however, immigrants from other regions of the world moved into New York City, specifically immigrants from mainland China (Zhou & Lee, 2015). Upon their arrival, Chinese immigrants were immediately segregated and excluded from most economic activity within the New York region, leading to the creation of "Chinatown" in the city. This zone was heavily populated by Chinese immigrants, but threats existed from outside racial groups. In response to segregation and these racial threats by other racially identified gangs, Chinese gangs emerged to provide protection for their members from said rivals. At the same time, *tongs*—similar to trade organizations—developed in order to provide economic advantages and opportunities within these communities. These tongs soon became the center of labor and everyday life within the Chinese community.

Gangs transformed within the New York region while still somewhat localized to this zone throughout most of history. With the final expansion of gangs within this territory from the 1930s to the 1980s, shifts were seen in the gang's dynamics and operational goals. Decker, Gemert, & Pyrooz (2009) suggested the industrial revolution and shift of industry and production within the United States fueled the migration of individuals from rural and isolated communities to major city outlets. This mass migration, however, was problematic as those moving from these remote locations lacked training or education to compete in the workforce and were limited to manufacturing jobs. Gang activity soon spread throughout other boroughs of New York, reaching outside of the historic gang localization within Manhattan to include areas of Harlem, as well as the Bronx and Brooklyn (Howell & Griffiths, 2015). Indeed, the introduction of Jim Crow-era laws and hostilities towards Black Americans in the South drove a mass migration of Blacks to New York and the surrounding areas in order to escape prejudice and racially-charged crimes. With Latinos further moving within these territories, New York began to transform its ethnic profile. This drove further race conflicts within localized slums that these individuals were forced to live in. As a result, gangs emerged as a way to provide economic and physical protection for their members in these regions.

Gang expansion was also further pushed through the early 1900s and reached the Midwestern United States, most notably Chicago, Illinois (Howell & Griffiths, 2010). "Organized crime" became part of life in Chicago with mob bosses such as Al Capone monopolizing Prohibition-era illicit activities such as bootlegging. At the same time, Sicilian-based gangs were emerging in these new markets during the 19th century with steady economic development through illicit activities including gambling and racketeering (Hagerdorn, 2005).

Similar to the New York expansion, Chicago was also riddled with its own challenges as Black Americans migrated into this territory (Hagerdorn, 2006). The enactment of Jim Crow-era laws also affected Black community members who raced to escape the growing tensions in the south from Whites who committed heinous crimes against Black community members. As a consequence of the mass migration and the racial divide that also existed within the Chicago area, Black community members were driven into centralized locations with those of the same racial identity. White gang members at this time focused on Black community members, at points driving through Black communities to perpetrate "drive-by" shootings. As a result, Black gangs were created in order to provide protection for their community. Migration patterns among Latino individuals also occurred in this region. Latino gangs emerged in a similar fashion as racial tension and violence flared throughout the city. Gang wars and rifts based on racial identity became problematic and continue to exist today.

In all of these regions, shifts occurred in the way gangs operated during the 1970s and 1980s (Hagerdorn, 1998). This era was primarily driven by the introduction of crack cocaine throughout the United States (McLean, Robinson, & Densley, 2018). Further shifts in operational means were further driven through the increase of the availability of firearms in the United States, the effects of revolving prison-door policies, increased economic motivation, and shifts in society that prioritized economic success as status, which particularly appealed to disadvantaged youths. Indeed, gang members were primarily motivated to join gangs in the pre-1970s as a means to protect individual members and their associated group, but this changed with shifts in culture and criminal justice policy, and economic motivation became intertwined with the gang itself.

Los Angeles Gangs

While Los Angeles has been affected by the growth of gangs in a similar fashion to that of the rest of the United States, the history of gangs within the Southern California region is unique in the changes of landscape within this region (Howell & Griffiths, 2015). California is unique in comparison to New York, where gangs emerged in areas that were predominantly populated by White individuals. Indeed, California has combined historical roots both in US and

Mexican history. After the Mexican-American War, California was acquired by the United States and soon after entered statehood. Prior to this period, California was an independent republic in its own right and was invaded and occupied by the United States. After the acquisition of California by the United States government, Mexican citizens found themselves under the domain of the United States and remained in their homes.

With the migration of White Americans into California, Mexican-Americans were restricted to the areas they had previously occupied. Compounding the presence of Mexican-Americans in this region was the mass migration of Latino individuals, primarily from Mexico (Telles & Ortiz, 2008). The 1900s marked a large expansion with a growing demand for laborers, primarily driven by the creation of railroad systems connecting the Eastern United States to the West. As the Mexican Revolution caused uncertainty and created economic difficulties within the country, many Mexican individuals moved to California to find opportunities in the economically booming city of Los Angeles. Many of the Latino individuals within the greater Los Angeles area were restricted to their own segregated communities called *barrios*. Groups formed in these barrios as protective entities for these communities, operating to an extent in a similar fashion as a street gang (Howell & Griffiths, 2015).

Two racially charged events that occurred in the 1940s further drove the call for protections of Latinos within the Los Angeles region: Sleepy Lagoon and the Zoot Suit Riots. The Sleepy Lagoon murder and its subsequent trials caused Latino community members to become outraged by the lack of integrity in the investigation and prosecution of a murder within the greater Los Angeles region in Commerce (*People v. Zamora, 1942*). Sleepy Lagoon originally involved the suspected murder of a Mexican-American male and subsequent investigation erroneously concluded that 25 members of the 38th Street gang, a Latino gang, had attacked and murdered the victim. In response, media reports concluded individuals wearing zoot suits, a loose fitting and baggy suit of the time, were associated with the murders as this was attire generally attributed to gang members. During the subsequent proceedings, over 600 Latino males were indiscriminately arrested by police for alleged involvement in the original murder case. Of these, 17 Latino youths were charged with the murder. The trial was riddled with due process issues and violations of the accused members' rights under the US Constitution. For instance, the defendants were barred from properly communicating with their legal defense team and were ordered to appear in their "zoot suits," which at the time were primarily associated with gang members. Furthermore, prejudicial testimony with no true value was allowed, spoiling the jury and painting an unfair portrait of the defendants. The case resulted in twelve guilty verdicts against twelve defendants, but upon appeal they were overturned.

    The Sleepy Lagoon murder led to growing racial tensions within the Los Angeles region, in particular hostilities and animosity that developed against Latinos primarily by White individuals (Howell & Griffiths, 2015). In the immediate days of the full on emergence of the Zoot Suit riots, an altercation between Latino "zoot suiters" and off duty US Navy sailors broke out in which a White sailor sustained a broken jaw. The violence of this instance was further amplified by the growing trend against these individuals, in particular as servicemen had previously started to target individuals of the Latino community wearing Zoot suits, indiscriminately attacking them as they saw these individuals as being engaged in criminal enterprise. On June 3, 1943, the riots officially began with a group of sailors departing a bus and targeting individuals wearing Zoot suits, engaging in verbal assaults that eventually led to physical altercations. Over the following weeks, more service members flooded the streets of Los Angeles, targeting all those they suspected to be involved in gang activity, specifically those in the Latino communities. These attacks eventually spread to other locations in the United States with Mexico eventually pleading with the United States government to end the violence and filing a formal protest with the US State Department.

Latino gangs went through a secondary stage of evolution throughout the 1960s and 1970s, specifically as a result of shifts and changes that occurred within the United States (Howell & Griffiths, 2015). Economic opportunity existed within the United States for Latino immigrants, specifically in farm work and other service industries. These industries garnered greater support and development through the Chicano Rights Movement, which in turn generated shifts in the way Latino gangs had to respond to economic and cultural problems that had existed in prior times. Furthermore, the War on Poverty made it more difficult for Latino individuals to escape racial disparities and move outside of poverty, creating a greater demand for protections within these communities.

Black-affiliated gangs have a different history in context to Los Angeles and their development than their Latino-based counterparts. Black gangs emerged and developed in the Los Angeles region during the expansion of the Santa Fe Railroad, which provided economic opportunity for those who sought to escape the economic hardships and disadvantages of the South (Vigil & Taylor, 2012). At the same time, however, those migrating to the Los Angeles area were still faced with the challenges that they faced in other regions of the United States (Howells & Griffiths, 2015). Discriminatory practices were routine within the city, forcing Black individuals to move to predominantly Black communities.

As such, White community members and gangs focused their attacks on Black communities, such as those that occurred with Latino communities and White race relations (Alonso, 2004). Discriminatory practices and emergences of "White Clubs" led to an increased amount of confrontation between these two ethnic groups. With the emergence of the Civil Rights Movement, however, "White clubs" started to decline in their numbers, allowing for another evolution within the Black gang community.

The 1970s and 1980s also ushered in a new era for criminal enterprise for both Latino and Black gangs (McLean, Robinson, & Densley, 2018). Crack cocaine became a widely available commodity in urban city centers throughout the United States, becoming a primary commodity of trade for the Black gang community. At the same time, and through the past few decades, the United States also saw marijuana drug trafficking and sales as a primary issue among Latino gangs. With the rapid popularization and availability of these drugs, gangs started to see further expansion both in sheer volume of those within the gang life, while also providing an economic escape from poverty for these gangs and their members.

Multicultural Perspectives on Gangs

Gangs have been widely seen as operating only within racial identity (Simon, Ritter, & Mahendra, 2013). Indeed, gangs have been found to have separate identities that are rooted within their own social context and racial identity. At the same time, however, the expansion of gangs within the United States has also led to different variations in the compositional makeup of gangs as certain gangs form rivalries against gangs of the same ethnic identity, for instance MS-13 rivals the 18th Street Gang while both are identified as Latino-based gangs. The rivalries within the context of similar ethnic gangs have led to an increase in partnership with other ethnicities within certain regions. Rather than Black gangs having a rivalry against all Latino gangs, extrinsic networks and truces are formed that allow Black gangs to be at peace with Latino gangs through deals to work with one another. This, however, is limited in research and gangs still are typically divided amongst their own racial divides in the composition of the physical gang itself.

Differences emerge in the values and general operation of gangs across racial lines, especially with Black and Latino gangs. Black gangs have been notoriously divided amongst two primary gangs: the Bloods and the Crips. Alonso (2004) theorizes the deep differences between these Black gangs have been primarily focused on injustices that have occurred within the Black communities and as a response to embedded racism within the most social and legal systems within the United States. At the same time, these gangs operate as a means to help provide a sense of belonging and protection for gang members (McLean, Robinson, & Densley, 2018). Through the introduction of crack cocaine in the 1970s and its overflow into the gang markets in the 1980s and 1990s, Black gangs have seen economic rise to an extent as this has created a financial market for them to engage in. At the same time, this introduction of drugs within the market has led to wars within Black gangs as they compete in the same region with violations of territories occurring. These gangs, however, are aided through national networks of fellow gangs, especially in terms of affiliation with Bloods or Crips. The identity of a Blood or a Crip, however, does not fully protect a Blood from a Blood or a Crip from a Crip as different factions have been created within these gang organizations.

Latino gangs are operationally unique in that their formations do not reach only beyond state borders like Black gangs, but also have their own unique expansion. With the evolution of gangs, Latino gangs have become transnational gangs with connections and gang affiliations in other countries. MS-13, for instance, is a Latino-based gang with affiliation and connections in El Salvador (FBI, 2016). As such, youth members are specifically recruited in order to further the mission of the MS-13 and link to other networks within El Salvador and the MS-13 operations in that country. Unlike Black gangs, however, MS-13 and the 18th Street gangs are not primarily focused on economic enrichment in their territory and protecting territory per se. These individuals have the gang become part of their family, focusing on providing for the gang and enriching the overall mission of their gang.

      Research, however, has indicated that the large proportion of activities that gangs engage in are rather benign. Members' daily activities are not riddled with illicit activities. Rather the gangs primarily provide a social "hangout" (McLean, Robinson, Densley, 2018).

Chapter 2

Community-Based Gang Intervention and Outcomes

Ashley Fortier, M.A. & Liane Mitchum, M.A.

In the county of Los Angeles, there are an estimated 1,000 gangs with 88,000 active members (Serjeant, 2007). The impact of gang-related activities and crimes has human, economic, and quality of life costs. The damage spans much further than just individuals; it also disrupts the wellbeing of the community. It has been found that violent crimes in Los Angeles are disproportionately perpetrated by gang-involved individuals. The Los Angeles Police Department estimates that nearly 40% of all robberies, 40% of all aggravated assaults, and 80% of all homicides are gang-related (Crime Mapping and COMPSTAT, 2010). Even more staggering is the estimate that 75% of California's total gang-related homicides can be traced to Los Angeles gangs (Dunworth, Hayeslip, Lyons & Denver, 2010). The fiscal cost of gang-related activities is said be to nearly $1.1 billion per year (Rice, 2007). With an estimated 300,000 at-risk youth in Los Angeles, many of whom have witnessed or been victims of violence making them susceptible to gang recruitment, the potential for this problem to magnify increases substantially (R.A.C.E., n.d.). This is why many gang prevention programs enacted in Los Angeles target at-risk youth before they become gang affiliated and perpetuate community damage.

The Community-Based Gang Intervention Model was developed in order to increase community safety through addressing gang violence in a comprehensive and cost-efficient manner. As an integrative approach, the

Community-Based Gang Intervention Model provides services that address the systemic and institutional barriers faced by gang-involved youth and their families in their day to day lives (Cardenas, 2008). There are four primary goal levels included within this model, each level focusing on a particular aspect contributing to gang violence. The first level focuses on violent crisis and life-saving efforts. The second level focuses on establishing and maintaining peace within the community. The third level focuses on factors that cause violence towards self and others. The fourth and final level focuses on building a non-violent environment (H.E.L.P.E.R. Foundation, 2012).

In order to receive federal funding for a community-based gang intervention program, there must be a minimum level of services provided (Cardenas, 2008). These baseline services include street mediation, developing local and regional truces, peace agreement maintenance, and crisis prevention. Other baseline services include evidenced-based mental health services, job training, development, and placement, removal of gang-related visible tattoos, juvenile/criminal justice support and alternatives, as well as educational support and services (Cardenas, 2008). These baseline services ensure that a minimal level of intervention has been met and allows for such services to be adequately measured in terms of their effectiveness.

A unique characteristic of the model is that it adopts a two-prong approach to gang violence reduction and the delivery of services. The first prong calls for the need of peacemakers placed within the communities to prevent and mediate conflicts, respond to crises, and provide rumor control to avoid escalation of conflict or retaliation between gangs (Cardenas, 2008). As a result, gang intervention specialists are placed within communities to promote public safety through the reduction and prevention of gang-related and gang-motivated violence and crime. The second prong of the model calls for the delivery of rehabilitative services to gang-involved individuals, their families, and their communities. Services such as mental health services, career/job training, development, and placement services, gender-specific services, LGBT services, sex and drug education services, recreational services, juvenile and criminal justice support services, independent living and housing services, tattoo removal, educational and support services, arts and culture services, and faith-based and indigenous services (H.E.L.P.E.R. Foundation, 2012).

This model also offers a variety of social development services that aim to improve the lives of gang-involved youth, their families, and communities. Re-entry, relocation, and transition services help individuals reconnect with their families, friends, and community while ending their time in custody (H.E.L.P.E.R. Foundation, 2012). The goal of these services is to help individuals successfully transition back into their daily lives without relying on "underground economies," which bring harm to themselves and others (Cardenas, 2008). Advocacy services are also provided in order to ensure that individuals, families, and communities have the rights and resources that they are entitled to. Advocates aid individuals, families, and communities to access legal, educational, health, housing, transportation, and other needed resources (Cardenas, 2008). Safe Passage and Safe Journey Programs are provided to ensure the safety of children, youth, and other community members as they move throughout the community, with a focus on the paths between home and school. Through these services, sanctuary sites such as churches, schools, shelters, and non-profit centers are identified so individuals can escape domestic, school, and street violence situations (H.E.L.P.E.R. Foundation, 2012).

Youth, Community Organizing, and Mobilization services are provided to engage the community, specifically the youth, to examine their world, identify key problems, develop solutions, plan and implement campaigns of change as well as create policies, programs, or institutions to address such problems (H.E.L.P.E.R. Foundation, 2012). Mentoring and Training programs help establish respectful relationships between youths and adults which foster guidance, knowledge, and direction. The goal of these mentoring programs is to empower youth to achieve their aspirations and to establish non-violent relationships with adult figures (Cardenas, 2008). Detention, Prison Visitations, and Outreach services provide a variety of services and are delivered in juvenile halls, jails, ICE detention facilities, youth camps and prisons, state and federal prisons, as well as court-mandated placements (Cardenas, 2008). Lastly, there is a Public Policy Development component of this model, which focuses on developing or reforming existing juvenile justice and youth development laws and legislation which, in turn, impacts public policy pertaining to prevention, intervention, and incarceration of youth, families, and communities (Cardenas, 2008).

Four methods are typically implemented to combat gang behaviors and crimes: prevention, intervention, suppression, and re-entry (Best Practices to Address Community Gang Problems, 2010). Community-based gang prevention efforts largely target youth who are at-risk of becoming involved in gang-related activities. Prevention is one of the best economic avenues for change-making as this approach prevents crime before it begins. There is substantial evidence supporting intervention at the youth level. Research has indicated that gang recruitment tends to begin around age 10 (Gang Reduction and Youth Development Newton GRYD Needs Assessment Final Report, 2010). Effective programs targeting youth must involve age appropriate material and focus on eliminating motivations for initial gang involvement (Guilfoyle, n.d.). Commonly cited motives include involvement of friends, family, and neighborhood; desire for protection; respect or power; perceived boredom; monetary gain; and to attract significant others (Gang Reduction and Youth Development Watts/Southeast GRYD Needs Assessment Final Report, 2010). In addition to reducing motives, gang intervention programming should provide community alternatives to the streets to promote more prosocial lifestyles.

In an attempt to address community violence and prevent youth and young adults from participating in gang activity, the city of Los Angeles has developed a number of programs to decrease community violence overall. Established in 1986, People of Community Involvement (P.C.I.) is a non-profit focused on gang prevention and intervention, job referrals and training, youth education and recreation, and food distribution for low income community members (P.C.I. People for Community Improvement, n.d.). Part of the P.C.I. mission is to promote social responsibility and personal accountability.

Reclaiming America's Communities through Empowerment (R.A.C.E.) is a non-profit based in West Athens and Gardena in Los Angeles County (R.A.C.E., n.d.). Its mission is to provide community development for at-risk youth and their families. Programs include youth sports, job training and placement, social and park safety, mentorship for boys and girls, gang prevention and intervention, after school programs, and alternative sentencing programs.

Another community gang intervention and prevention program is Advocates 4 Peace and Urban Unity, which is a non-profit located in South Los Angeles and committed to "bettering the lives and infrastructure within Los Angeles" (Advocates 4 Peace & Urban Unity, n.d.). To prevent gang violence, Advocates 4 Peace & Urban Unity provide safe passage programs for children, school programs for families and children, and enrichment classes in local elementary schools (A Better LA, 2016).

Brotherhood for Independent Leadership through Discipline (B.U.I.L.D) is a comprehensive non-profit focused on gang prevention and intervention through youth empowerment. B.U.I.L.D provides services to vulnerable populations, including all-inclusive victim services, grief-response-stress management, personal achievement courses, violent behavior management courses, high-risk youth modification, and safe passage services (A Better LA, 2016). B.U.I.L.D also aids in the re-entry of previously incarcerated individuals into the community. Additionally, B.U.I.L.D promotes personal growth through advanced educational literacy services, adolescent and adult mentorship programs, survival life skills services, manhood and womanhood developmental intensification programs, tutorial guidance and youth education services, along with specialized job training and placement programs (A Better LA, 2016).

Founded in 2007, Inner City Visions focuses on gang violence reduction and youth development in the Florence-Firestone area of Los Angeles. Inner City Visions takes a peacekeeping stance through assessing gang threat levels and preventing gang conflict and recruitment. Like the previous organizations, Inner City Visions offers a variety of services, including violence interruption and conflict mediation, community crisis intervention, street mediation, rumor control, creating and maintaining cease-fires, intervention organizing, and family advocacy for victims of violent crimes (Inner City Visions, 2016).

Toberman's Gang Prevention and Intervention Department in the Harbor Area of Los Angeles was one of the first gang intervention programs in the area (Toberman Neighborhood Community, 2014). Beginning in 1977, the organization has been committed to increasing the safety of the community through cost-effective gang intervention efforts. All staff are certified gang interventionists per the two-pronged approach. The overall program goal is to build a "peace infrastructure."

Professional Community Intervention Training Institute International (PCITI) is another intervention organization. It was created in 2006 to train and certify gang-intervention specialists (The Professional Community Intervention Training Institute, n.d.). It provides multi-level certification trainings as outlined by the National Intervention Certification Board (NCIB). The program is organized on two tiers: classroom instruction and real-work interactive scenarios. The interventions provided include violence prevention and intervention, situation-specific training, critical incident response, crisis prevention and planning, gang intercession training, safe schools and passage instruction, safe community advocacy, and subject matter expertise. Since the PCITI began, over 15,000 individuals from varying fields and backgrounds have been trained.

It is crucial to provide at-risk youth and gang-affiliated communities with safe and healthy alternatives in order to effectively combat gang problems. Summer Night Lights (SNL), which is a community-based program, offers just that. The program extends park and recreation hours throughout Los Angeles during the summer months (Summer Night Lights Program Overview, 2011). The philosophy of this program is that by opening parks and community areas during prime gang-related activity times and providing safe, prosocial activities, the number of children drawn to gangs will be reduced. The program began in 2008 with eight parks, but has since grown each year. As of 2011, 32 parks in LA were participating. During that same year, it was estimated that 710,000 people participated, 11,000 people per night were served food, and an extra 1,000 summer jobs were created. The results of this effort have been positive. It appears that SNL has been a constructive outlet for youth and that it has strengthened community bonds.

While gang intervention is difficult to study due to the complexity of investigations, known results of intervention programs have been staggering. Just in the Los Angeles area, the R.A.C.E program claims to have reduced the murder rates in West Athens by 70% since 2008. From 2016 to 2017, Inter City Visions achieved a 43% reduction in violence and murders within the Florence-Firestone area, as well as a sizable reduction in crime and violence in local schools and the community overall (Inner City Visions, 2016). In an attempt to reduce violence, Inner City Visions provided a peacekeeping presence in local schools, parks, and within the community. Inner City Visions eased tensions between gangs through counteracting and dispelling rumors that would incite gang violence and retaliation (Inner City Visions, 2016). Inner City Visions successfully created "safe zones" in the community where youth can enjoy gang-free recreational activities. Furthermore, Inner City Visions prevented predatory crimes and violence against students going to and from school in order to promote safe passage for youth within the community. When prevention and intervention efforts succeed, there is a clear economic advantage. Successful prevention can substantially reduce the high costs of police officers, gang task forces, medical bills of victims and supplementary victim support services, legal proceedings, and incarcerating offenders (Guilfoyle, n.d.). In particular, juvenile programs have been fiscally beneficial. It has been estimated that prevention programs that target juveniles have the most consistent economic returns compared to other forms of gang and violence prevention efforts (Aos, Phipps, Barnoski & Lieb, 2001).

Their Stories

Chapter 3

Anthony "Ant Dog" Porter

The gangs were still forming in Inglewood in the mid to late sixties, sprouting from the roots of the civil rights movement. The neighborhood I grew up in was called "The Bottoms," a wide swath of concrete carved out of the map from Century Boulevard to 104th Street and Crenshaw Boulevard to Yukon. There I was, at the center of this pivotal shift in history, in the middle of The Bottoms, Century Boulevard and Imperial.

My elementary school years were spent at Center Park Kelso Elementary School, across the street from the Forum where the Lakers used to play. Most of my friends in those days were white. I had a few Black and Latino friends, but in the early 1970's, there weren't many of us in the city of Inglewood. That changed in the mid-seventies. The demographics of American cities changed, and so did Inglewood's.

Discipline and respect were not optional. We had to respect our elders. We had to figure out the way of the world – sink or swim. The newspaper route was my first step into the real world. It was the perfect learning experience for a kid. I had to wake up early. That took discipline. People expected their paper to be at their front door when they woke up. That demanded responsibility. And I had to work hard to make a dollar – capitalism. It laid the foundation for all the principles I thought I needed in life.

As the city changed, so did I. The contentment of childhood passed, replaced with the angst of adolescence. I went from throwing papers to throwing fists. My father was in prison, so it was just my sisters, my mom, and me. I was still a baby myself but I had to be an adult. I tried to provide for them but a paper route isn't going to cut it when you need to support a family, and there wasn't much work available for an eight-year-old kid – so I stole. The first time I was arrested I was ten years old. I was picked up for petty theft: A skateboard for my sisters and me and a flashlight for the family in case the power went out. Shortly after that, towards the end of junior high, I began hanging around with some of the older guys in my neighborhood. We called ourselves Bloods.

Inglewood is known for Bloods, more so than the Crips or any of the Hispanic gangs. The Bottoms was the epicenter of the Bloods in Inglewood. We were youngsters. We didn't quite understand what we were getting ourselves into. It came naturally. It's like when you're a baby, you crawl and then one day you stand up and start walking. Then you go to school and start reading. These progressions happen without us thinking about them or willing them into being. Gangbanging was the same process for me. At the time, I thought this just happened in my community. It wasn't until I was older that I realized this thing was much larger than my neighborhood. It's going on in hoods across the world. By the time I was old enough to realize the deadliness of the situation and the deadliness of the organization I was a part of, it was too late. I was too deeply involved.

Once the violence began, it was swift and without reprieve. The first time I became involved in this new way of life came in the seventh grade while I was at Monroe Junior High School. There were citywide riots between the Blacks and Hispanics, and our battleground was school. Our school popped off into a full-blown riot. I got caught blindsided by a blunt object, which busted my head open, requiring several stitches.

The violence between the Blacks and Hispanics in 1979 was reaching an impasse. There was so much tension that we did not go to school for weeks. Schools could not have us in the same place at the same time. The violence was on sight. It got so bad that it went beyond fighting and rioting in the streets and hallways. People knew where each other lived. They would show up at a rival's door, and someone would end up injured or dead. The gangs were still forming and you had a lot of young kids out there trying to prove themselves. There was never a moment where I could relax or let my guard down. Even when we were allowed back to school you had to worry about being killed. That was the turning point where I became full-fledged.

Then I started getting locked up. Weapons possession, firearm possession, in and out of juvenile halls until I was eighteen. Then it was in and out of prison. Along the way I had ups and downs marked by profound pain and loss. I was shot, my mother was shot, my sisters were shot, and I continued to live that way of life. It became normal to me; the only life I knew. The chaos burned bright, and I was attracted to it like a moth to flame. I did not pay attention to the signs of death and destruction that lay ahead. I ran my own program.

My father was in prison and my mother was a tiny lady so there wasn't much she could do. I was always respectful to her, but I did things my way. The homies were always at my house. They could hang out all night if they wanted to, and my mom never said anything. She was thankful we were in her home instead of running in the streets.

As I got older, the pursuit of hardcore gangbanging activity lost appeal to me. I faced a lot of time and spent a lot of that time staring at grey walls of prison cells. I lost the desire to hurt people. I realized people who were labeled my "enemy" were living the same lives as I was, enduring the same struggle. They were people who were just trying to make it; who were trying to outlive expectations; products of their environment trying to survive this juggernaut we were all a part of – just like me.

Then in 1998, I lost my son while I was incarcerated. The darkness and solitude of losing a child is something that few understand. It is a chill that runs through the fabric of my soul. Guys lost parents and friends in prison all the time. They couldn't be there for their families because they were incarcerated. But there weren't many guys who lost kids while they were locked up. It is the worst thing that can happen to a human. It defies the rhythm and rule of nature. Children bury parents. Parents don't lose kids.

My son's name was Antoine Damu Porter. When I heard that he died, I felt the air rush out of my body and soul. It struck me that I may have cursed him from birth. His middle name, Damu, means "blood" in Swahili. I speculate whether by naming my son Damu, God saw me directing him into the same lifestyle that I was living. The cold truth of the matter is that sometimes I catch myself thinking that God took him away from me, that I cursed him with the name. I never had the chance to hold him.

That is what it took for me to start questioning my decisions. I was shaken up after that and started slowing down. It was still a struggle, and I went in and out of prison several more times, but from the day I lost Antoine there was something inside of me pulling me to change. But there is no getting out, no retirement plan. It doesn't matter how many people you lose.

Instead I had to change my programming within the life I was living. I wanted to be part of the solution, not the problem. With that key of willingness I believe God allowed me to unlock the door to my own personal freedom. Ten years ago he introduced me to PCITI. I was on the street and kept running into people who told me I needed to check out the course that was offered. Some were Bloods, others were Crips, but regardless of where they were from, they all told me about the community interventionist class. They said I had the potential to push a positive message and create change within the community. It was the exact message I was looking for, at the intersection of the perfect moment in my life where I was willing to hear it. People saw there was a chance for me to change. They recognized the urgency of the moment. The door is open only briefly and once it shuts it may never open again. They told me that the community needed guys like me who live the life, walk the walk, on the front lines, that the youth will only listen and respect a person who comes from their struggle. What they said reminded me of a man I met when I was locked up at fifteen years old.

It was during one of my first long term stints in juvenile hall. In my memory, my surroundings, the officers, the cells, and the other prisoners are all blended together in a mental rotation of incarceration environments. But one man always sticks out like a lighthouse in the fog. He was an older Latino who worked at the prison. I never saw him in a guard uniform, and he never carried a gun. He wasn't there to guard us. He was there to talk to us. He was a man who came from the same life we were living. He had the same affect and spoke the language that we did. He walked like us, ate like us, talked like us. We were kind of shocked they would let him work there; he seemed more like the prisoners.

We were youngsters, and the guards would try to talk sense into us, or just plain try to scare us straight. Of course, we didn't listen. We couldn't listen to them. We couldn't relate. But we could relate to this old man. He wasn't a do-gooder coming to preach his sermon. He'd walked our way of life, and all he did was tell us about his process of change, and that a positive way of living was available to us. It was a simple message, really. The messenger made it potent. I left juvenile hall, and that man faded into a memory. The only thing I got from him was the idea that I would like to do something for kids one day. When people asked what I wanted to do when I got older, I told them I wanted "to work with kids who messed up."

With so many people telling me to check it out, I decided to give the PCITI class a chance. In the beginning I scoffed at the idea of training. What did I need training for? I know this life inside and out. You would be hard pressed to find someone from my neighborhood who represented like I did. But after the first class, I understood.

We can't operate from just a street mentality. Street mentality alone causes chaos and discord. We have to have a professional point of view on the situation. The work we do need to be handled by professionals. I learned protocols, and they gave me a structured template on how to carry out intervention work. You can think you have all the answers, walk into the middle of a war and get yourself killed. The who, what, where, when, and the standard operating procedures are critical. The art of what we do comes with the balance of the street and professional sides of operation. I came into PCITI ten years ago and I have been an active part of that organization ever since.

Once I got involved I received guidance and structure. Most important of all, I found hope. I threw myself into a positive way of living, surrounded by good people who had the same purpose. Together, we set out to share our message to the communities we serve. We organized baseball and football games between rival neighborhoods and gave everybody a friendly venue to bond over common recreation. We set out to talk to the youth about living a positive lifestyle and gave trainings to community stakeholders.

We provide trainings on a catalog of different subjects. First aid procedures, CPR, crisis intervention, gang violence training, domestic violence training, seminars on issues affecting our community and brainstorming sessions

36

to solve those issues are just the surface of what we do. I would encourage any community stakeholder – shop owners, ministers, first responders, teachers and anyone else who has a social interest in bettering the community – to take our classes. They are not just for ex-gang members, community interventionists, or those working directly with youth who are involved in gangs. Our service is for the benefit of everyone.

Community transformation is another component of what we do. PCITI goes into the community, finds out what they need – resources, jobs, training – and assists them. If we cannot help directly then we guide them to the people who can. Our effort boils down to providing hope to our community and leaving it better off. We created chaos. Now it is time for us to clean it up.

For the kids, our primary message is one of respect. The kids don't listen to their parents but they will listen to us. They are so caught up with the image of a gangster that they are receptive to those who lived that life. The message is to get the children to listen and respect their parents. The other side of that is parents need to be involved in their children's lives. We see fifteen and sixteen-year-old kids who are living on the street. The best defense for keeping a youth out of a gang, and the best predictor for a child's success is the involvement of their parents. We hope to close the gap between kids and their folks and open the lines of communication that may be closed due to lost respect.

This new way of life requires us to be all in. One foot in the door and one foot out will not work, like trying to build a façade before laying a foundation. I am still in the street. That is where I will be effective. The difference is instead of perpetuating negativity and carrying out harmful actions, I spread the message of a positive way of life and carry out actions that will make my community better. Disconnecting or getting out of the life means turning my back on a community I helped to destabilize. I scorched the earth for many years. There is no getting out and walking away. I have a responsibility to clean up the mess I created. I protected my community with violence. Now I protect them by trying to change the lives of the children in it, saving them the brutality I had to go through.

    I hope to get as many people in the community involved in this social change as possible, until it spreads like a fire to other communities so we can prevent these killings and start saving lives. That's where I am at today. It is still a struggle. The work is ceaseless and the phone rings constantly, but the work has to be done. We cannot keep killing each other off. I want better for my life, my children's lives, my community, and the world at large. The only way that is going to happen is if guys like me start giving back.

Chapter 4

Barbara Jett

I moved into the neighborhood when I was in the fifth grade. Gangbangers lived across the street from us. I was the eighth child of nine and life was pretty normal. You wake up, go to school, come home, eat dinner, go to bed, wake up and do it all over again. The monotony broke when the guys from across the street threatened my older sister. I rolled up my sleeves and walked across the street with my chest puffed out, chin up, to tell them that this wasn't going to be okay. They busted up laughing, pointing, saying, "Look at this little girl!" A couple of years went by. As I got older, my fire grew hotter and my tongue sharper.

I was in a fight at Southwest College. A girl hit me in the head with the teeth of a metal comb. The stem was stuck in my head, blood running down my face. The sound of sirens broke the haze of combat. Police dispersed the scene and sent everyone in different directions except for a group of girls. One of the girl's mothers took me to the hospital and got me sewn up. They said they were impressed with how well I fought. They did not tell me who they were but I knew. This group was a clique who ran with one of the local gangs. My fighting skills proved I was an asset. Through my act of violence I won over the affirmation of this new group of peers. A gangbanger was born.

My family life was normal. There is nothing in my past that would earmark me for the path I took. It was your average American childhood. I did not join a gang because I was lacking something at home. The girls I met after the fight looked like they lived life fast. They had an edge that I identified with. After the twilight that came with being accepted into a large group of peers wore off, the regular business of robbing and beating people, and stealing cars commenced.

At first it was petty thefts and robberies, small time stuff. We were in a store off of Imperial and Prairie and robbed the man at the counter. He locked us in the store so we couldn't get out. We didn't let him call the police. Instead, I picked up a chair and threw it through the window, giving us the opportunity to escape. We ran through the streets of an unfriendly neighborhood in turf that we were not supposed to be in. Just when it looked like we were stranded, my homegirl's mother just happened to show up – like she always did we were in trouble – as if she had a Lo-Jack system on us. She whisked us back to the safer side of town as we were rolling with laughter over the events of the night.

Life in the streets moved along and so did the violence. A poignant memory for me is the night Crystal's brother was shot. Crystal is now an interventionist, as well. We were at the roller skating rink. A fight broke out and gunfire sent people darting in every direction. As we ran away, that same friend's mother spawned out of the night sky once again and we took off. Crystal's brother was shot in the eye and blinded for life. When violence is not premeditated, that is how it usually goes. People argue, someone pulls a gun, and one of them winds up shot.

I graduated from high school because my mother would not accept anything less. I had to gangbang on my off time in those days. I never went to jail because my mother was a probation officer. When I got in trouble, they would call her and send me home. When I turned eighteen, she stopped bailing me out and I started going to jail. Theft, burglary, possession of a handgun, firing a handgun. I repeated offenses and repeatedly went to jail until the judge got sick of seeing me and sent me to prison.

I can honestly say prison was not that bad for me. I can adjust to whatever situation I am in, but I remember being terrified when our bus pulled up to the gate. My heart was beating fast; so fast and forceful it felt like it dragged me off the bus by the neck. The razor wire looked like it wanted to jump down from the gates and slice you. The walls were towering behemoths of stone and steel. Inside the prison I didn't recognize many faces from my neighborhood, but I knew plenty of enemies. I was able to navigate the politics of prison with a calm, strong, steadfast disposition. People left me alone and I did the same. My two-and-a-half-year sentence can be described as uneventful – a monotony of three meals a day, spades, reading, writing, and gossip. I witnessed some nasty things that women do to each other, traumatic events that I am thankful I never went through – hot curling irons and shaved broomsticks shoved into sensitive areas, women fighting over sexual partners, rape, the most beautiful woman you have ever seen shave her head and sag her pants so she can look more like a man. I stayed out of that mess because I was never into those things, but that is life in a women's prison. The next few years were a carousel of women's camps and jails – in and out four times.

Incarcerated women from San Diego to Bakersfield are sent to Chowchilla, and Bakersfield north to Valley State Prison. They are across the street from one another. I, a southern girl, found myself in VSP, where I didn't know a single warm body. I found a few SoCal girls in there, mostly women who were pregnant – VSP is where they send pregnant inmates – but in the end prison was again uneventful, a different carnival, the same carousel. Three meals a day, spades, reading, writing, and gossip.

Everything was fine until I came back to my neighborhood. I came home to a rolling tide of change. New girls came up while I was away. Their experience was much different than mine. I was appalled at the way they allowed themselves to be treated by men, and in turn how they treated each other. No one addressed each other by name, it was all "bitch" and "ho" talk. I was not raised like that and no man or woman ever spoke to me that way either. When I joined, they told us to dress properly, conduct yourself with respect, and act accordingly. If you broke the rules or were disrespectful, there were swift and sudden consequences ranging from beatdowns to death. It was all about respect – of others and self. When I returned, I witnessed the new generation tearing their women down.

In my neighborhood they run through women, and they run through them fast. Women come into the life looking pretty decent and in a matter of months they look old and used. One story in particular sticks out to me. I pulled up to one of the hangouts and from the view on the street it was pitch black inside. It looked like the house was abandoned. I walked up the steps with the feeling of skepticism in my gut. When I opened the door, the lights were off. I hit the switch and saw a bunch of young girls on their knees enclosed by a circle of men standing over them. The men had them performing oral sex on whatever stranger was in front of them, rotating until the men were through. I was disgusted. I made the girls get up and we went into the living room. The men fussed and complained, which I could understand, I blew up their spot, but then the girls started barking at me too. They were mad at me for stopping the whole thing! I tried to explain to them that they were worth more, but I was getting nowhere. I left the house frustrated, discouraged by the degradation. I couldn't shake that cold realization of the truth – that those girls did not want to believe they were worth more. That is when I discovered how hard it is to instill self-esteem and self-respect into someone who has none.

Witnessing the way those men treated these girls was my reason for change. If they treated them the same way they treated me, then I am not sure if I would have done anything different. I didn't change for me. I changed for the gang. I could not live in alignment with the way they treated women. I would not allow myself to be treated that way and I would not accept it.

A big reason for the change is that the women are not what I call "soil." They aren't home grown, from the neighborhood. Men aren't disrespecting and dehumanizing their friend's sister, or their old schoolmate from elementary school. People catch a Greyhound bus to Los Angeles, come into the hood looking to be a part of something and are allowed in. Women from all over the place end up in neighborhoods they didn't grow up in, and they get taken advantage of. The personal element of growing up here is lost.

Another reason is the lack of requirements. There are none today. It used to be that we required you fight; you were willing to rob people; that you had enough heart to put in the work required to earn your stripes. I was treated as an equal because I was willing to put in the same work. I went along on the robberies and shootings; I earned my keep. Now it is all about getting jumped in, which is another thing I never understood. If you hit me, we will never be friends, and you will never be able to trust me. In the past it used to be that if your family was in the gang, you would be grandfathered in, now even family members have to be jumped in.

When I came home, I was so discouraged and disheartened by the things I saw, the changes that had occurred while I was away, that I wanted to do what I could to restore order. Coincidentally a friend of mine, T-Rogers, sent me to Aquil's class. It was the perfect moment in time. I was willing.

The first day of Aquil's class, I walked into a conference room, set up like a classroom, with rows of chairs and long tables facing a whiteboard. We sat waiting for class to begin when from behind a wall we heard arguing followed by the unmistakable sound of heavy gunfire, like thunder rolling through the building. I saw some of the biggest, scariest gangbangers jump and run for cover. Some hid under the table, a pair went in the bathroom and locked the door, one was trying to climb out of a window. It was mayhem. Five minutes prior to this, they were talking about how hard they were and what they did in the streets, "I did this…" "Ima do that…"

The argument and gunfire was fake. Aquil had put us in this situation to see how we would react. That is how he taught us. We can all say what we will do. Anyone can talk to the tough bravado, but attitudes and actions change when it is live. I fell in love with the class, particularly because it was scenario-based. That was the best way of teaching me. Aquil put us in all sorts of unconventional situations to see how we would react in the moment. Along with the scenarios, and equally as pertinent, was his emphasis on our mindset. He said, "The same mindset you had, the same energy and integrity you put into gangbanging, has to be the same as what you put into this." I took that oath, followed that credence, and applied it to saving lives.

When I was new, I had to earn my place within the intervention circle. It was not a given. T-Top, who is a good friend of mine today, called his connections in my neighborhood and ran my resume. He wanted to make sure I was who I said I was. It checked out. I proved myself with good intervention work and fast in the street. They didn't just let me walk in the door; they made sure my license to operate was legitimate. I kept coming back to PCITI and was told Aquil would never let a woman on the team. Less than a year later I was a member. Then Aquil put together a women's intervention team.

After I graduated, I brought some of my homegirls to take the class and tried to send the ripple further along. Those who took the class are doing wonderful today. Some time passed and I ran into Crystal. She told me that she had taken Aquil's class, as well. During our conversation she mentioned to me that she wanted to do something for the people on this side of town. I agreed and we did some good work with the people in the community, but the hardships I witnessed little girls endure continued to erode me. I wanted to reach these girls.

Even with all the positive things I was doing, I got caught up in a situation two years ago. It occurred after a 'hood day, a neighborhood block party. As I left, I tried to get my nephew to leave with me but he refused. He wanted to go to the hotel for the afterparty. I knew the people he was going with were not his friends. It didn't sit well with me. I could sense that this was going to be a problem later, but I let it go and went home.

At four a.m. my phone rang. The voice on the other side asked me for a fade – a fight. I would handle it. Here is where I went wrong. I referred back to old behavior. Right before I walked out of my house, the idea struck me that I better bring protection in case this went sideways, so I packed a gun, a Taser, pepper spray and a knife into a fanny pack. I went back to the hood pissed off and ready for an altercation. They wouldn't come out but I could hear them laughing behind the paper-thin motel door. That sent a rage through me. I put my gun through the window and told them my nephew was going to come and open the door for me. Screams bellowed from inside the room. "Oh my God! Barbara Jett! Barbara Jett! She's got a gun! Oh my God!"

I took a deep sigh. This was going bad. I had to act fast and de-escalate this situation. I calmly replied, "I didn't come here for this. I came here to get some keys." I put the gun away and asked them again for the keys. They were so worked up they couldn't function. It seemed that this was going nowhere, ominously heading towards a violent end until suddenly, the keys came flying out of the window and landed on the deck. We went to leave and when I heard from behind me, one of the guys scream, "Blocc Crip!" I felt that rage return and surge through me. I barked back, "This is all mine. All of this is mine. I built this." No one wanted to fight so I left. When I got home, I felt the weight of what I did and the opening of scars. I had put myself in a position to inflict violence. The old behavior returned, if only for a brief moment, and the discomfort ran through my body like a current.

If I was going to continue my work and be effective, I had to let go – of all of it – the old behaviors, the discomfort, and the anger. I feared I would lose my place in PCITI, but I sat down with Aquil and we worked through it. I came out of the other side with a stronger bond to Aquil and the work that we do. I became hypervigilant of situations I am in and more aware of myself. We work hard to re-route old pathways of beliefs and behavior, but the old ones lay dormant. One snap decision or impulse and those insidious behaviors return. That was the last time I ever harmed anyone.

One thing Aquil makes very clear is that we have to survive the streets. We still live in the neighborhood. Around every corner store or building façade could be danger. He teaches us how to survive. He says, "There is no P in interventionist." I am an interventionist. I am not a punk. My skill set remains the same. That is true for all of us. Will I rob someone again? No. Do I still have the ability to hurt someone? Yes I do, but that is not my intention today. But I will defend myself.

At this present moment I am working as a case manager. The gang interventionists go into the streets and find people who are gangbanging due to their circumstances, that if their lives were different they would act different. That is a difficult task as there are some people who love the life, the thrill of gangbanging, and would do it regardless of their situation. But there are others who believe that it is the only way they can earn a living, survive in their neighborhood, or be successful. For the latter group, the interventionists bring them to me. My team and I try to direct them into a safer way of life. We provide job training, life skills training, financial literacy courses, the tools with which they can navigate the world in a positive way.

The site I am working at now is in a neighborhood that my crew used to war with. When the kids found out where I was from, they were disrespectful and did not trust me. I met them where they were at and brought the intensity to them. When they called me names, I dished it back. They have to know they can't walk over me, otherwise I would be ineffective in my work. I received one of my most difficult cases early on. He was a teenage boy who thought he had it all figured out. He would call me "nap" – the insult for people from my neighborhood – all day long. I pegged him as fearful and without direction, which gave me the extra reserve of patience and compassion I needed. He went through all of our training and I still keep in touch with him today. He no longer calls me nap. He calls me Ms. Barbara.

The job we do now is personal. It is about human connection. What I do is ninety percent talking. It is about getting to know the people I serve, their unique situations and needs. If I think I can help them, then I guide them to the appropriate resources. Some will tell me right off the bat they want to go to jail for the rest of their lives. But the ones I can connect with, I say, "If you followed me when I was doing wrong, I need you to follow me now and do things differently." I didn't know if I would be dead by now, but I knew that I would be in jail for the rest of my life. The fact that God reached down, put his hands on me, and showed me a new way of living makes me want to give it away to anyone who is willing to walk with me along this narrow path.

A number of years after taking Aquil's class, I finally set out on my journey and joined a 501(c)(3) called Phenomenal Angels of the Community. Phenomenal Angels was founded by four women from Underground Crips who work specifically with at risk and gang-affiliated girls. We mentor girls between the ages of seven and seventeen, empowering them to change the course of their lives. We provide the same life skills and financial literacy education that are offered in the other programs. Additionally, we teach self-defense courses, body image and self-esteem seminars, and domestic violence education. We provide them with the opportunity to have different life experiences as well. Some of the girls have never been bowling before, so we take them. Others don't know that ocean water is blue because they never saw the ocean. Up until now their worlds have been very limited. We try to open their world up. A key component of our program is teaching the girls how to give back. Community service is mandatory. After our body image and hygiene unit, the girls put together beauty and hygiene bags and pass them out to the homeless. We keep the girls under our guidance and care until they are eighteen, and those who go through the entire program leave better off than when they arrived. None of them are actively gangbanging. Since our inception six years ago, out of the hundreds of girls we've taken care of, only three have dropped out.

Now that it is summer, those of us who do intervention work need to be on the top of our game. When it is hot, we pray for the rain. The heat affects people in a strange way. As the temperature rises, fuses are shorter and triggers squeeze easier. Decisions are made in an instant, and the pause between life and death evaporates. During the warm months, I try to throw community events on days where gangbanging may be an issue. If the community is outside and together, fear and violence are reduced. For the interventionists, it means we are outside from sunup past sundown. Messages and politics move quickly in the streets, and we have to know what is happening, when it happens.

I have the highest admiration for the guys I work with in PCITI. When I first joined, they were on their best behavior. They acted like gentlemen. I thought it was hilarious. I had to tell them to close the curtain on the show and be themselves. We are all the same. I just wear a dress. All of the guys are wonderful, beautiful people, and they have come to my rescue countless times. They have given me guidance, and they always answer the call. There are certain neighborhoods I cannot enter because of my affiliations. Sometimes I need an escort. Aquil, in his brilliance, picked the team so that he can cover the entire city of Los Angeles. From the Valley to the Westside, we have interventionists from every area of the city.

It is all about presentation for me. I have to be able to walk into a room full of men and have their respect. I won't do that that on my knees, and I won't do that on my back. In order to work with PCITI I need to possess the same integrity and values as the men. That is what I try to instill in these young girls.

I say you can gangbang if you want too. I still hang out with gangbangers, some are in my family and some are my friend's children. Whether they continue to gangbang or not is their decision. It is a part of our daily lives. If there is a 'hood day I am there. Gangbanging is something that is never going to end. But what we can do is restore a condition of self-respect, a sense of community, and a safer, more positive way of life for these girls and boys.

Chapter 5

James "Blue" Marks II

I grew up with my mother and sister – raised by all women. I remember as a young child, I would wake up early in the morning and wait for my father to come home. He never did. When I was growing up, my mother's boyfriend was physically and emotionally abusive to my sister and me. We would be driving home from school and for no reason at all he would turn around and smack me in the mouth. We would walk by each other in the house and he would open-hand hit me in the head. There was no rhyme or reason to it, no discipline behind it. I could not understand or wrap my head around it. As a result of the abuse, I could not trust anyone. My life felt like it was confined to a small box.

When she was only twelve years old, my grandmother gave birth to my Uncle Clifford. Clifford was an Army grunt who became a violent heroin addict during his time in the military. He left a wake of chaos, wreckage, and dead bodies that forced our family's exodus to California. He was the oldest male in my family and took the role of patriarch. The way he disciplined us did not require physical violence. He would make us hold books over our head until our shoulders gave out, or do pushups and run sprints until our arms and legs could not handle it anymore. He was tough and we all respected him, but his heroin addiction took him in and out of our lives.

We moved to the Carmelitos housing project in Long Beach when I was about ten years old, and that is where I was exposed to the open wounds of society – drugs, gangs, and violence. My auntie was a drug addict with two kids who my sister and I used to babysit while my auntie was running around in the streets. She was gone most of the day, and my mother was constantly working so we had free rein to figure things out on our own. I'd hang around in the projects and picked up a love for breakdancing. My friends and I brought our cardboard boxes to the center yard of the projects and would dance for hours.

Then I began to witness violence that piece by piece dismantled my sense of safety in the world. My Uncle Clifford beat my aunt with a belt for not changing my sister's soiled pants quick enough. He beat her right in front of my sister and me. We were blown away. It put the fear of God right into us. I never saw a human being beat another grown adult like that before.

As I spent more time at my aunt's house, I saw how frequently she wore fresh scars of violence. She was a beautiful woman and had several boyfriends, but they only showed up on the first and the fifteenth when the checks came in the mail. In the weeks after they came around, she would have black eyes and swollen lips. She was always suffering abuse at the hands of men. It made me think that this kind of violence, especially violence towards women, was normal.

I was ten years old at the time and didn't know exactly what was up with my auntie, but I knew she wasn't right. Even at that young age, I knew normal people who had it together did not experience such constant calamity as she did. This was all confirmed one summer's day while my sister and I were hanging out at my aunt's house. We were sitting in the living room watching cartoons when the sound of a boot busting through the wood door shattered the calmness of the morning. Three men and two women came in shouting, "Where that bitch at? Where she at?" They took a look at my sister and me and stomped right past us towards the staircase. I recognized them as our neighbors who lived across the grass yard.

The group went upstairs, found my aunt in the bedroom and proceeded to beat her. From downstairs I could hear crashing into the walls, my aunt's screams, whimpers, and hands violently contacting with flesh. The woman shouted, "Bitch, where my money at?" All I knew to do was run upstairs and try to help my aunt. One of the men in the group cut me off midway up the stairs and showed me his gun. He stood higher than me, holding the weapon steady, inches from my face. My sister grabbed my arm and hid behind me. I was completely powerless, with my innocence torn from me right there in that moment. I said to my sister, holding her tight, "When I get older, ain't nobody gonna ever be able to do us like this again."

I never realized until much later in life that much of my involvement in gangs and violence was a result of trauma. I did not know what trauma was, let alone believe that I suffered from it. It was only when during one of my intervention classes that I realized the impact trauma had on my life. I told the teacher about my abusive stepfather, my aunt, and the violence I witnessed growing up, and she told me that I had suffered trauma. I never looked at it like that. But I was never the same after those men and their sisters came into our house and beat my aunt.

Long Beach was my home, but I was going back and forth from my mother's to my grandma's house in Compton, down the street from Compton High School. During my adolescence I became enthralled with the dangerous, edgy, side of life. I remember at the time I was reading *Blue Rage Black Redemption* by Tookie Williams, a notorious West Side Crip from South Central Los Angeles. I'd look out my window and see guys like him and King Rat with big afros, real buff, hanging around the empty lot across the street from my grandma's house. They had an aura around them that was so potent, I could feel it hit me in my chest as I watched them from my window. They were untouchable in a neighborhood that was dangerous, even deadly, to so many.

My mom worked several jobs, and one of them was a graveyard shift, so I'd stay at my aunt's house a lot of the time. She would be in her room getting high with her boyfriend, not paying any attention to me, and I'd slip out of the window ledge, down the laundry pole, and out onto the project streets. That's where I would go to the basketball courts where the guys in the neighborhood hung out, playing ball, selling dope, and hanging out with girls. I got my start with them by being a lookout. I'd watch out for the cops, and that's how I got my pass. That was my way in.

When I started hanging with those guys on the court late at night, it became all I wanted to do. I loved to breakdance and I lost my interest in that. I didn't want to do anything that wasn't furthering my street reputation. I grew older and got the pass to hang out with the guys more frequently, during the day. We would hang around all day drinking Thunderbird and Silver Satin with Kool Aid aka Crip Juice, bumping the boom box. I thought I had made it! Here I was, a young teenage kid hanging with the established gangsters in my projects.

Then crack came into the picture and swept through like a virus, decimating entire families and neighborhoods. I witnessed grown adults committing utterly demoralizing and disgraceful acts to themselves, all in the name of the drug. The power drugs had over people tripped me out. Mother and fathers would abandon families; people would kill each other just for the next fix.

But the OG's in my neighborhood were like celebrities. When you saw them out in public, they had that same energy like when you see someone famous. Their presence had depth and weight, and they were surrounded by money and women in our neighborhood where poverty was rampant. They embodied the messages of manhood that young boys receive from society: be emotionless, be a womanizer, be dangerous. In the more affluent neighborhoods these messages may have meant something different, in my environment it translated to being a gangster.

My first real orientation into the life was through an older cat named Roger Parks aka Killa Mush, a big time drug dealer in the projects on the east side of Long Beach. He took me under his wing and would take me on joy rides around the east side. We would pass by another kid around my age – thirteen years old – and Roger would say to me, "Go hit him in the mouth. You from the projects. He can't fuck with you." Just like that, no explanation behind it. And I did it. I didn't have the role models and wasn't taught the principles to be able to not hit that kid in the mouth. Roger had kids of his own, and at night he was locked down in his house. I began running dope for him. I would take the money from the fiends and slide it through the steel bars of his door. He would pass the drugs back to me. My homies and I did this until the sun came up. When the day broke, Big Fred Dog would come by, and we went to Reid Probation Continuation School. We hoped that an enemy would check in so we could run into the class and give him a beatdown.

I was also hanging around with a buddy of mine, Marv, who was my age, but more advanced in this way of life than I was. We hung around the eastside and the kids over there were already running around with guns committing robberies and armed burglaries. They were cowboys, and I instinctually stepped my game up. The thought that I was getting into something serious never crossed my mind. It was like a video game and I was leveling up. We had a loyalty, a brotherhood. I never had any brothers growing up so the closeness and camaraderie I felt blotted out any fear of incarceration or death. It felt real. I lived it and was willing to die for it. That was the allure the life had on me.

My first shift in perception came when I was incarcerated as a kid. I got locked up for beating my sister with a baseball bat. I was released and locked up for crimes in rapid succession until I landed in the California Youth Authority, where I stayed until I was twenty-one. It was in the CYA that I first read *Detroit Red,* a book about the life of Malcolm X. That book changed my perspective on life. That man went from a street kid to one of the greatest leaders of the 20th century, and his story of transformation showed me internal change was possible. Where I came from, addicts were found overdosed in the alley and gangsters lived and died by the gun. No one was talking about changing their lives. It was considered an honor to go through the rites of passage of probation camp, CYA, prison, and inevitably die for the things we did, either in the streets or on death row. When I was released I went back to the streets, but a seed was planted.

Three years after that moment in CYA, I was on the run for an accused double murder and attempted homicide. I had a daughter that I was not present for as I was dodging the law. I thought I was going to die in a cell, my daughter the only legacy I leave on this earth. That story of camaraderie and brotherhood proved to have holes shot through it when one of my own OG's snitched on me to the authorities in Long Beach. I went to prison, but what I thought was the worst day of my life, turned out to be a blessing. Certain police officers had knowledge that the word was out to kill me. Also, if it wasn't for that act of betrayal, I never would have received the knowledge and education that watered the seed Malcolm planted in me nearly a decade ago.

During that trip to prison, I met two men who would change my life forever for they showed me the path to internal freedom. The first was this guy Mack who couldn't read or write. We would sit down in the common area together and I taught him phonics and the alphabet. He learned how to read and write, and in turn, taught me about blackness. Blackness is the emotional and spiritual bond that connects African-Americans, based on a common history and common experiences. I never looked at the world through this context before. I had always felt I was on a spiritual journey and was always looking to be a part of something, but I never identified with any common experiences other than the gang experiences I shared with men on the street. This was bigger than that, and I began to see the reality of how small my world really was.

The second man I met during a stint in the hole. He used to slide me literature under the cell. He'd slide me a piece of paper, sometimes for no longer than an hour, tell me to internalize it and then wake me up in the middle of the night and make me recite it. They, too, were about this concept of blackness. They were about being a warrior, and the struggle we all faced. He educated me about the soldiers that came before us and paved the way, and now it was our duty to do the same for the next generation. Some of it was abstract, poetic-type reading, but on the whole they were a collection of principles. I found strength and self-esteem in those principles. They motivated me to be a soldier for the light, as oppose to the darkness I was shrouded with. He talked about a collective oneness and love of my fellow man. I think, above all, he genuinely cared about my wellbeing. He was wise, and saw the broken families and communities that were left in the wake of broken men. He provided me the tools to better my life and did not want anything in return. This was a revolutionary experience, contrary to all the principles and experiences I was handed growing up. He gave me my Swahili name, Hakika Bomoni Askari (True Warrior Soldier), a name I would eventually give to my son, Askari. He told me to internalize it, breathe it, become it, live it.

I looked back on my life, and I saw the first time God introduced himself to me. I was a young kid, thirteen years old, and at that time, every summer, my mom would send my cousin and me to our grandad's house in Texas. The bell would ring on the last day of school and we would jet home. The next day we would be on our way to our grandparents. While we were down there, we bounced around various family members' homes – different aunts and uncles – but I loved staying with my grandparents the best. My grandad was my best friend. When I was there, they would butter me up, always feeding me well and giving me money.

One of those early summer mornings, I woke up early and heard my grandad and grandmother talking in the kitchen like they usually did. The tone was different. There was an air of uncertainty to it. I heard my grandmother say to my grandad, "I need you to go to the store and get eggs, milk, bread, and lunch meat. I need the eggs and milk for breakfast tomorrow, and I need the lunch meat and bread to feed the kids." He responded, "That's all the money we have until we get paid." Those words were a rock sinking to the bottom of my gut. The way they treated us, we never would have imagined that they had any worries about money. I did the only thing I knew how to do at that young age. I got on my knees and said a prayer to God. I said, "God, please let me find some money to help my grandmother and grandfather."

I was always a hustler. I've always had a job, ever since I was young. Back in California, there was this white guy named John who used to come to the projects to sell flowers out of his big old Ford van. My friends and I would help him sell the flowers and made a couple hundred dollars for the day. Then we'd go to the Paramount swap meet or Sears in downtown Long Beach and buy brand new khakis, Converse shoes, and sweatshirts. But then we got greedy and stuffed the money in our socks and told John someone robbed us. So that was the end of hustling flowers with John. But in Texas, the only money I had coming in was pocket change from a newspaper route I was running.

As noon came around, I heard my grandmother call out to grandpa, and tell him to go to the store to get the groceries. I walked into the room about the same time and grandpa said to me, "Hey, Pistol." He always called me Pistol. "Want to come to the store with me?" "Yeah," I said. We hopped in his old, banged up pickup truck my cousin kept in the corner of the yard and went to the store. The whole ride there and during our time shopping I felt uneasy and anxious. It hurt to know my grandparents were going to struggle.

We did our shopping and left, and as I walked out of the store I stepped on something large. I thought it was a rock at first. But it was too soft to be a rock; it gave gently under the weight of my foot. I looked down and saw a roll of money. I stopped, I said, "Daddy! Daddy!" I called both grandads "Daddy" because my father was serving a life sentence. I saw his face, confused at first, turn to elation. He said, "Grab it! Grab it! Jump in the truck!" I picked up the roll mid stride and started for the truck. As we peeled out of the parking lot, I said in jubilation, "I prayed for this! I prayed for this! I heard you and Momma Jesse saying y'all have no money!" At the time I could not connect the dots on what that moment really was, a direct blessing from God.

Then I began to look back for other moments in my life where God was there for me. There are so many. One came to mind from when I was on the run. I was staying on 54th, at the house of this woman everyone called "grandma" because she was like the grandmother of the hood. They all knew I was on the run, but they were hiding me, taking care of me. I was over there one day smoking weed and sherm, doing whatever it was we were doing. I had to run to the store, and as I left I asked Grandma, like I did every time,

"Do you need anything?" She responded enough times with "ice cream" that I started bringing it over for her every time I came by. Several times, there would be a bunch of old ladies in her bedroom having a Bible study. The old ladies all knew I was on the run for murder and would say prayers for me. They never judged me or called the cops on me. I felt calm when they were reading that book and eventually when I came over, I'd go in the backyard and say, "What up?" to the homies, then go to Grandma's room, hop in bed with her, and read the Bible to her.

One time I will never forget, she put her hands on me, looked me straight in the eyes, into my soul, and said, "Son, you know you're gonna be caught one day. But when you do, I want you to do one thing for me. When you get caught, every morning when you wake up, I want you to say the 23rd Psalm. I want you to say that at lunchtime and before you go to bed. When you get on that bus before you go to court, I want you to say the 23rd Psalm. Before you walk in the courtroom, I want you to say that. Before you go in that holding tank, I want you to say that." I religiously did that, and I beat my case. I have one Bible tattoo on me and that's the 23rd Psalm, "The Lord is my shepherd, I shall not want."

My journey has been a spiritual one. I beat the case, got out of prison, and continued doing what I was doing on the streets. This time around though, I had a feeling I needed to get away from the guns. They amplified every situation a hundred fold. They made every routine argument life and death. I left the house with three to five years in my pocket every day. I continued with the drug dealing but I was far from the cowboy that I was prior to going to prison. This was a shift for me because I used to love guns, like really love guns. When I was little, Uncle Clifford would blindfold me and make me take apart and reassemble guns. I had storage units full of them. I had those big grandma-sized purses that old ladies carried around filled with bullets and clips. I had footlockers full of weapons. But then I faced the most difficult spiritual test of my life. It crumbled and distorted my entire reality: my oldest niece was murdered.

My girl picked me up from the airport; I was returning from out of town. When we got home, I checked the answering machine and heard a message from my auntie. All she said was, "Your baby got killt. You need to get over here to your mom's house." I was like "what?" I couldn't believe it. I was in a state of shock and denial, but in my depths I knew it was true. So we ran over to my mom's house. I came in the door to a living room full of my family, sadness sketched on everyone's face, a grey energy settled in the room. She was murdered. They found her in a house in San Bernardino dead two days with a bullet through her eye.

I had taken care of her and let her stay with me for a while before she died. She was smoking weed, was in and out of the streets. Sixteen years old and when I took her in, she was living at some thirty-year-old guy's house, running the streets with him. My wife and I let her stay with us and set ground rules and curfews – be back by dark kind of thing. We tried to establish some sort of discipline for her. It was all good for a while until other members in the family put her on a bus to Las Vegas where she ended up running the streets. We came home one night and she wasn't there for curfew. I called the local hospitals and police stations for two days asking if anyone had seen her. We were the last to know that she went to Las Vegas. She moved back in with my sister and her husband who were strung out on drugs. I was furious and that's when we had a falling out. I had not heard from her until I heard she was dead.

I experienced deaths in the family before – my grandparents, my uncles, my great grandmother, and countless homeboys. My response was always, "Okay, how much do you need for the funeral?" Shell out the cash, take care of the loose ends, and get back to the business of the streets. Death never fazed me until I walked into that house after my niece was murdered. All I could say to my family was, "All I ever tried to do was try to get her to avoid her doing something stupid like this. Now all this shit has to come back to me. I'm the guy that got to go out and handle it." It all fell on me. I still didn't know what happened, didn't know she was sitting dead in the house for two days. I saw the pain and sorrow that my family suffered. Something had been taken from us. I looked at my Uncle Rockhead, her dad from original Compton Crips Oaks Park aka Santana Block, and I could see in his eyes that we had the same thought. It didn't matter what neighborhood this was in San Bernardino. We were going to go out there and gun everything down, and then every year on her anniversary, we would go back, and gun everything down again – women, men, it didn't matter.

  I walked out of the house and paced with this darkness and wrenching soul pain inside of me. I knew I had a decision to make. I don't know if it was that day or the next day, but I called my brother in law. I told him that he needed to meet me at the storage. There he told me the situation. They were at war with the Mexicans in Wilmington. I told him firmly that all I wanted was to maneuver the game and not have to hurt anyone. I gave him the gun I had. The only way God could get my attention was through my niece. She was the only one who could affect me, and 'til this day, she was the only one who could call me Uncle Blue – the rest of them could only call me Uncle – we were that close. In that moment I felt that I was being tested in a spiritual way, and I gave up all my guns.

  After my niece was murdered, I was tested again when my grandfather died in Texas, and again when my uncle died of a heroin overdose. My wife caught a federal case up north and I was traveling back and forth to see her. These tests started the change in me. I gave up my weapons.

I didn't have access to large amounts of cash anymore and thank God I didn't, otherwise I might have been paying people to harm others. But with no cash and no guns, I wasn't willing to go out on the streets and do the things I used to in order to get money. That was when it hit me that change was occurring within. I started to lose fascination with the game. As I sat and thought about it, once the money went, everybody started to fall away. It was an inner purge. A lot of people in my life just fell off. What I was not expecting was my wife to start slipping away. I thought she respected how I got money and not the money itself, but that wasn't the case. So I came through the other side of losing both of my best friends – my grandad and my uncle – my wife, and my niece, and I started to feel for the first time in my life. Emotions came rushing in that I had suppressed since I was a kid.

Despite everything I went through, even when it seemed that God had turned his back on me, I never stopped praying. I prayed for that purpose – that I would find mine in life and carry it out. It came when Jerome, aka J-Dog, signed me up for a class on community intervention. It was an intervention class for ex-bangers like me. I felt that quiet inner voice speaking to me, a slight nudge, and I stumbled in here. I started seeing people helping one another, and I was connected with mentors and some solid homies who showed me how I could use my experience to help people in my neighborhood. These were guys like T-Top, Geer, OG Mad Bone, Eight Tray Gangster who I had done time with as a youth in CYA. They said, "When you do something, and you know that is what you're supposed to do, you will know." That quiet inner voice speaks. It got my attention. So I did what I was supposed to do – help others – and I started to feel better. I began to see value in myself, and my past. It was the currency I could use to help other people moving forward. Just as important, I developed compassion and understanding for the situations and trials of life that others are going through. I have sympathy for others now. Before I was ruthless – no mercy.

Every moment from the past leads to this one, and without any one of them, this moment would not exist. What I realize now, is that I had always been doing the work I was called to do. My life on the streets prepared me exactly for my life now. I was always the guy in the hood who was helping people out. Someone died – "Here's some cash to get you by." A kid got good grades – "Congratulations, here's a hundred bucks." "Your grandma can't pay the rent? Okay, send me the bill." I was always like that; I was always helping people. I had that in me all along. The transformation came from that great loss I experienced. Those moments of trial bridged the gap from where I was to where I am now. There are not too many people left from my era who can sit and write these words down on paper for you.

Chapter 6

Nikko Deloney

I was born along the Wilshire corridor on the Westside of Los Angeles in 1969. The early '70s were the years of Evil Knievel, and I had the AMF '76 Evil Knievel bike. My life was normal in those early years, simple. My father wasn't around, but my mother did well for herself as a singer and an actress. You might have heard her singing the "ooo-OOOO-ooo" part in the background on Joe Cocker's "With A Little Help From My Friends" or as a voiceover on "Josie and The Pussycats." She was the breadwinner for our family and provided a nice life for me. The generations that came before us, especially the grand folks, looked out for us. They tried to instill in us some structure of morals and values. My grandmother was in the background as well, providing the guidance and wisdom that the older generations possess; the ones who have weathered more than a few storms. Those older folks, even the hustlers, would let you know when you were buying into a game you didn't belong in. They would tell you, "This just isn't for you, kid." As the years went by and as I witnessed family systems erode due to drugs and violence, those voices became whispers, growing fainter as with the ticking of time's clock. Until the mid-1970's, I had some semblance of an average American life. I was just another kid cruising down Fairfax on his Evil Knievel bike, taking it off the cuts in the curb, imagining they were 60-foot ramps with school buses underneath me.

Then Grandma started taking care of everything. Mom became more distant and absent and as a boy I didn't have the tools developed to understand why. When she was present, she wasn't in her right mind. I was six or seven years old when I first got in touch with that emotion of anger. What

I didn't know at the time was that I was witnessing mental illness and drug abuse. All I saw was Mom coming and going, leaving in one mental state and returning in an entirely different one. My uncle suffered similar circumstances. He came back from Vietnam with a part of his mind still lost in the jungles of Southeast Asia. Between him and my mother you could see happiness, sadness, and anger in the same conversation. A lot of violence came with that, and I saw its effects on the family system early on. Within me, the seeds of anger and resentment had been sown, and like any seeds in fertile soil, they grew well.

Grandma became the main fixture in my life during those early years in the '70s. I was born with Blount's disease, which causes me to walk bowlegged. I've walked with a limp ever since I was a child. But nevertheless, I have walked. When I was young, the primary doctor I had seen my entire life up until that point told me I would never walk. When my grandmother was given that news, she snatched me up out of his office and took me to a specialist. I always thought my deformity was a result of my mother's drug use, but later on I learned that my doctor prescribed me faulty medication. Many years later he got sued for malpractice. That relieved a lot of the resentment and anger I had towards my mother.

But growing up, I was filled with both of those emotions. With my mom in the condition she was in, I had to learn to fend for myself. Grandma did the best she could, and the older generations possess a lot of wisdom, but a young man is going to follow the influences he sees around him. My influences were the violence and gangbanging going on around me. The Crips and Bloods street gangs were gaining strength in my neighborhood, and my developing mind was flooded with the images and experiences of hustlers, gangsters, police raids, and violence. Through my young eyes, I perceived the spirit of this life to be in the same groove as Evil Knievel. It was edgy and raw. These guys had money, power, and respect. Here I was, nine years old, practically raising myself, trying to survive, and watching the local boys roll down the block in brand new Cadillacs. I was placed in a situation I could not have had the tools to handle. During the day I would go to school and then come home to the responsibilities of being an adult. The conflicts with my mother got worse and with my family system deteriorating, I turned towards what I perceived to be an attractive alternative. I wasn't receiving proper input on how to live life from my home, so I turned towards the only other place I thought I could find it, the streets.

On the Westside the gang culture was present, it has always been present, but back then everyone just wanted to be the number one guy. It was no different than football teams, or prizefighters. Everyone wanted to be the best – the one getting the attention from the girls, with the nice car and big bankroll. Today it has all changed.

The 1980's meant the departure from the Evil Knievel years and the entrance into the Scarface ones. My mother was missing a lot, and when she was around abusive and devious men typically accompanied her. I was growing into manhood at this time, and I had a chip on my shoulder. She would bring one of these guys around the house, and I'd end up in a screaming match with her and a fistfight with him. My family wrote her and my uncle off as crazy. That is how the older generation handled those things. They didn't tell me too much about it. I wasn't sure if they were trying to protect me, or if they just didn't know how to explain it themselves, but that was as much of an answer as I got about them.

I found an early escape from what was going on at home in sports. I got involved in local athletics and youth clubs in my neighborhood. My friends and I would attend the Sugar Ray Robinson Youth Club, Police Youth Club, and Wednesday movie night with the police. The police actually used to pick us up and take us to the movies! At the youth clubs, they had a boxing ring and some free weights, and the officers would show us how to work out and take care of our bodies. We were mostly interested in the boxing rings and learning how to fight. Many of the kids in my neighborhood came from family systems just like mine. We were experiencing similar traumas and witnessing the same environment on the streets. Boxing was an outlet and we liked to release all of that anger we had inside of us. The way it shook out, naturally, was that kids from each neighborhood would band together and fight the kids from the other neighborhoods. A short time later these same cliques of kids would be shooting at each other over who could sell drugs where.

I found two other loves besides fighting and money – women and music. It is hard to say which has given me more problems over the years. I've almost been killed playing shows in the wrong neighborhood. At the age of ten I started playing the drums, and in eighth grade, a few kids from the neighborhood and I had our own band. We played all over Los Angeles at youth clubs, Jewish community centers, and Catholic school dances. I could grasp some moments of innocence behind a drum kit or in an arcade playing Galaga or Space Invaders, but even then I'd have to steal quarters from my mother's purse. It was never truly pure – few things in life rarely are. If you look at any clear blue lake long enough, you will see the sediment seeping in from the shore.

By the early 1980's I had traded my drum kit for turntables. I went to school at one of the roughest schools on the Westside – Louis Pasteur Junior High. This is where I linked up with some older cats who were DJing. It was the hottest thing jumpin' at the time, and I made a name for myself around Los Angeles as a musician. The days of the neighborhood kids and me boxing at the youth club turned into us gangbanging on the streets. This became a problem for me as I quickly found out I couldn't play shows in certain neighborhoods. House parties in Venice were out of the question, and if I wanted to come home with my turntables or my life, Crenshaw and Slauson were not happening either.

In 1984 I had a leather jacket and a Cadillac, and you couldn't tell me shit. I was a member of the Playboy Gangster Crips street gang. The same kids I went to youth club with, I was now running the streets with. Our rivals from the next block over or from across town became our sworn enemies. Those days were marked by looking over my shoulder and being on constant alert. Minor mistakes like being caught on the wrong block or mouthing off to the wrong person were fatal. Crack cocaine hit the streets in the early 1980's and an entire tide of societal problems, violence, and money flooded in with it. My crew carved out a niche selling crack and guns on the Westside and the rivers of money flowed freely for everyone. Personally, I loved guns. I loved everything about them especially the way the cold steel would turn hot in your hand as you popped off rounds. I got an adrenaline rush from it. In 1984 I got locked up the first time for shooting them. This marked the beginning of a long history of jail sentences for gun crimes – everything from selling them, buying them, and especially shooting them. I never got locked up for robbing someone with them though. That just wasn't my hustle.

The late 1980's and early 1990's were years of bloodshed. People around me began to drop off. It felt like one of my homies was getting killed every week.

"So and so got cut down on Main in Venice."
"So and so was stabbed to death on Vermont."
"So and so got caught for a double homicide."
"They gave him life."

It became such a routine way of life that I normalized it. News like that didn't surprise me anymore. It was expected given the circumstances of the life I was living. Every year – especially in the summer, I don't know why that is, maybe the heat has something to do with it – there would be a wave of killings followed by retaliations and then I would end up in jail. I'd get out, start banging again, and the cycle would repeat. I rode the carousel, and on and on it went to the tune of my own carnival of terrors. At the time it was just life to me. I was habituated to it.

Then in 1992 there was a wave of civil unrest after the Rodney King tapes came out. I was fresh out of prison for yet another gun charge and came back to the whole neighborhood on fire. You had to be there to understand the heat in people's hearts. Everyone was burning up with fear, disappointment, and anger. Especially anger. Honestly, we were all just tired. The people in the neighborhood were exhausted at the way the police were treating them, which had gone on for decades, mind you. The 1990's were just the first time we were able to record it on videotape. The kids were exhausted at losing parents to the streets and growing up in a state of poverty. The decade of crack had decimated entire family and community systems. Even the gangbangers were tired of killing each other, losing friends and family, and getting locked up for the rest of their lives.

Neighborhood leaders, police, gangbangers, and anyone else who wanted to come gathered in a local park and began the Westside Peace Process. There was a bond with everyone there regardless of who you were or what your job was. Whether you were a single mother, a business owner, a police officer, or a gangbanger, we were all there for the same purpose. We wanted to better our community. I sat across from guys who were my enemies and we made peace. Enemies became allies in this common cause, and while we always hated each other, we had a mutual respect for one another.

Shortly after this process, in 1993, I got caught up during a traffic stop and busted with guns again. I went back to prison. Back on the streets I had two kids and a third on the way. My mentality was that my kids were going to grow up in the gang culture just like their daddy did. That mindset was motivated by fear, and fear will have you acting in the most irrational ways, convinced that your perspective on the world is true north. I didn't want them to grow up in a different neighborhood and be stepped all over. I didn't want them to be used, robbed, or taken advantage of by predators. They were going to grow up in my hood, where they'd be taken care of. It is a twisted mentality but when you are in that position it is survival. I painted myself into a corner and had to do what I thought would be best for my family.

That mindset changed. I wish I had a good story to tell you how, but really I just got old. After I got out of prison it was the era of my sons and me. I wasn't a child anymore and the cycle of running the streets and getting locked up was worn out. As I matured, I saw that there was a ceiling to this kind of life. When my third child was born, my mindset of wanting to bring them into the gang culture flipped. I denounced that immediately with all three of them. I was lucky. My other two were still young and malleable enough where I could change their conditioning. I started to raise them with the same standards the older generations instilled in me as a young kid. I taught them respect and honor. I taught them that integrity was the crux of morality in a man. You have to have self-respect. I taught them proper grooming and to keep their hair and nails trim. Once a man has integrity and self-respect, then he can show respect to others. I was not perfect in my actions and while I planted the seeds of change in the next generation, my own personal change was a harder path to walk. Deeply entrenched ideas and concepts of morality had to be dug up and replaced. It is a slow process. In 1994 I went back to prison again for what I thought would be the rest of my life.

I'm sitting in the common area, contemplating what forever would be like behind bars. It was a messed up reality to look down the barrel at. Guys are playing cards in one corner, checkers in another. It's about an hour before the dinner chow bell rings. I take a look at the television and as fate would have it, Bo Powers is up there doing an interview on the news. I had a lot of respect for Bo from when we ran together on the streets. But Bo owed me money, and there he is on the TV! I was pissed. I could've used that cash on my commissary. But then something greater intervened, you could call it God, coincidence, whatever you want, but I stopped and listened to what this man had to say. Someone had just been murdered in his neighborhood and the newscaster was interviewing Bo. Bo was talking about these community interventions he was doing. He would go with a small crew into a neighborhood after a murder or during an uptick in gang violence and implement some strategies to restore peace again. He was walking the walk, right there on the front lines. It was the perfect cross of events between my new attitude I had in life after my third child, and seeing Bo on TV.

I called Bo from my prison cell. We joked about how he owed me money, and he told me that he's starting his own crew, that when I get out of prison I should call him and he'd get me set up. While I was serving the rest of my sentence, he sent me all kinds of literature about his community intervention team – pamphlets, books, and newsletters to keep me current on the situation on the streets. When I got out of prison at the end of 1994, I began my journey as a community interventionist. I served all of my time for every crime I was convicted for. I walked out of jail a free man and there was nothing left outstanding that could drag me back.

From 1994 to 2001 I worked directly under Bo as a community interventionist. We were doing alley and neighborhood cleanups, feeding the homeless and helping people find jobs. When violence broke out, we were in the middle of it trying to foster an atmosphere of peace. What we had that no one else did was our street credibility. We were recognized and respected in our neighborhoods. We all came from the same underbellies of that gang life. People listened to what we had to say because we were talking with them on a horizontal level, not down at them. We lived and breathed the same streets they did. We were not "outside help" or far removed do-gooders. We had to sleep here at night too.

I became a certified gang intervention specialist and violence prevention expert through the Professional Community Intervention Training Institute in 2006. PCITI is the only training institute that certifies people in community intervention. We work with emergency responders, law enforcement, educational specialists, social workers, and psychologists to provide community-based gang outreach intervention. The training I received there was hands on and specific to the scenarios we encounter on the streets. I was trained on how to manage an incident including first responder techniques, short term and long-term community outreach programs.

I get the feeling that when people think of gang outreach, they have the idea in their head that we just show up and preach our message to the guys on the block, hoping they will have a moment of clarity and see the light. It is so much deeper than that. What we are dealing with is generational and systemic. The gang mentality and its way of life is passed down from one generation to the next. It's what I almost did with my own kids. The second piece, the conditions in the community that incubate gangs and create an environment where that becomes a reasonable alternative are systemic. There are cycles of poverty and violence that have become interwoven in a community. Preaching does not uproot those systems. Tangible plans of action need to be put in place to change the conditions that keep a family, neighborhood, or city trapped in those cycles.

When a crisis occurs in a neighborhood, a gang-related murder of a young man for example, the first steps that need to be taken are life-saving measures. My crew will show up on the scene, sometimes before police or paramedics, and take measures to aid in saving lives. We all received first responder, life-saving training. In the wake of that crisis, short-term community peacemaking efforts need to be taken. This is when our credibility in the neighborhood is effective. We can reach out and talk to the necessary leaders and try to implement a peace treaty. Our goal is to prevent a full-blown war from breaking out. If short term peace is unobtainable, then there is no chance at addressing the long-term conditions that are creating this violence – the unemployment, poverty, and drugs, to name a few.

After peace is established, we can begin to address the violence the kids on the street carry out against themselves and others. We have to change the way they think about themselves and their neighborhood. A lot of these kids have bad B-movie syndrome. They think they are living out a gangster tale from *Goodfellas* or *Scarface*, but they are just the main characters in their own bad B-list movie. When I was growing up we had respect and honor. People took care of each other in the neighborhood. But the present situation is a bunch of cowboys running around. Kids just want to shoot at each other and get high because they hear it in music or see it on television. The heroin and opioid epidemic has made that worse. People are atomized and are only out for themselves. There is no camaraderie on the block. There is no rhyme or reason to any of the actions these kids are taking.

So we try to be the voice of reason. Not the voice of treason that they are hearing through their speakers or TV sets. Establishing a long term, sustainable plan for a community is our ultimate goal. We want to create an environment where people's thinking has shifted. Peace and non-violence become the important values to uphold. Many of these kids have lost one or both parents to the streets, or they grow up in a house with a single parent who has to work multiple jobs and is never home. They haven't learned basic skills like how to dress, eat, talk or act. We try to provide programs to show them how to do that, and outlets for them to express themselves with. We provide football and music programs for youth that I volunteer at. We also hold etiquette and grooming training for young men and women. It takes a community to raise a child and bringing the community together in positive action is what our whole blueprint depends on.

When I first got involved with community interventions in 1994, it was a trip to sit in a room, across from someone I swore I hated and see that we were exactly the same. We had similar upbringings and experiences and endured the same struggles. Take it one step further, and I saw that this person and I could work together towards a common goal. We both wanted a better community for our children and ourselves. Some days it is tough, to be honest. People are still killing each other, abandoning their children, and getting high. You wake up and wonder what you're doing. It can seem like you're putting your life on the line and giving this your all, and no one is listening. Part of my process was accepting that I am not capable of saving the world. I just do the best I can with the next person I come into contact with. Some are responsive and some aren't. But I know I have a steady heart and steady mind. I have no agenda. I am here to be of service – one thief showing another where to find bread.

Chapter 7

Tommie "Ttop" Rivers

I was born on the Westside of Los Angeles to a single mother. My father was absent in our lives. I had three sisters and one brother, and my mother worked two jobs to provide for us. She gave all of herself but she was not around a lot, working more than twelve hours a day most days of the week. I was fortunate to have almost a decade of that childhood glow, where everything is right in the world, and everything is good. I played baseball and football throughout my childhood and even though she worked a lot, my mother was in the stands at every game.

During my late elementary school years of fourth and fifth grade I acquired an acute awareness of my environment. My life became bigger than just the frame of my childhood and I noticed elements in its picture that began to intrigue and disturb my imagination. I saw poverty and people struggling around me. I became aware of the reality of life, that people had to choose whether to keep the lights on or put the next meal on the table. I also saw guys in my neighborhood that were thriving in this storm of instability. They had big cars, new clothes, and were surrounded by beautiful women. They walked with a sense of power and purpose. As I matured I saw that this kind of life was earned through violence, paid for in pain and violence. To make it in this way of life, you had to be part of a gang.

I tried to rush time and be a man. The problem was I had no male figure to model what being a man looked like. The message of masculinity I received was from gangbangers, drug dealers and pimps. I had no one to show me any other path. I didn't want to struggle and choose between bills and food like everybody else. I wanted money, power, and respect, a lavish and exciting life. It was an easy sell to a twelve-year-old boy who was filled with adventure and a sense of urgency, who thought he was invincible.

My environment slowly molded and influenced me. I saw my friends getting involved in gangs, so I did what every teenager does and followed the herd. I wanted to be a part of something bigger than myself. At twelve years old, I didn't know that there was no retirement plan to all of this. I could not foresee the future of violence and anguish that this life promises. I gave up my love of baseball and football and fell in love with the faster way. It would be a ball and chain to carry for the rest of my life.

I was the youngest in my family. My older sisters had boyfriends who were gang-affiliated. They hung around the house and I gravitated to them. I was interested in the older male demographic that was not familiar to me. I started hanging out with them every day and from there I knew I was in. Initiation to a gang came to me when I was in the fifth grade. A large group of us were out on the schoolyard and the older kids who were already initiated formed two parallel lines five yards long. My peers and I ran through the gauntlet and the older kids took their shots on us – fists and kicks, anything went. When I made it to the other side, I was one of them. There were no brakes or amber lights. I embraced this thing I had become a part of, and in the beginning it was a flood of new friends, action, and excitement.

I was infatuated with the money, the cars, and the lifestyle. It all turned out to be smoke and mirrors. The life looks enticing to youngsters, there's no doubt about that, but it either doesn't materialize, or in the marginally few cases where it does come to fruition, it comes at a heavy price – always ending with death or prison. The reality eventually sets in that all the money and cars in the world don't matter behind prison bars or under earth.

The mentality I had growing up was to be the best. I strived for that in every endeavor I took up. I wanted to be the best athlete, the smartest in class. When I joined the gang, I took it seriously. I applied that superiority complex to my new passion. It was a domain where my competitive personality was a shining asset. I was a born leader and now I felt that I was a leader in my community. 1986-1987 was the height of gangbanging. It was the era of Freeway Rick Ross and the crack cocaine epidemic. These were the times where we had to be the hardest, toughest individuals on the street. I held a sense of pride in the life I was living. I thrived on violence and putting in work. The mindset was to one up everybody else – be the toughest, the hardest, the most ruthless.

The life caught up with me at seventeen years old. I had just turned seventeen too. I spent the next ten years in prison for a crime I didn't commit. But because I was a part of a gang, had knowledge of the crime, and couldn't tell on anyone, I was tried as an adult. It was the price I had to pay for being loyal to my neighborhood. At that age, I didn't really understand the implications of the violence and crimes I was committing, the prison sentences that would come, the time that would be taken from me. Six months after being arrested, my son was born. That was the harshest part about the situation, but it was also a turning point. I knew something had to change. At the same time, I am young, incarcerated in a gang module, and facing a lot of time. My prospects for a different life were bleak.

I fought my case from county jail for three years, lost, and was shipped up to prison. Upon arrival in prison I caught a case and spent the next year and a half in the hole. For the first five to six years of my sentence, I watched my son grow up from behind glass, never having the opportunity to touch him. That was when it really impacted me that if I do not change, my son will relive the same struggle as me. The light came on just as I got out of the hole and sent up to Pelican Bay. That quiet voice from within said, "Now is the time for transformation." For the first time I was able to hold my son. I was still in prison but not behind glass. I felt the courage and conviction to try a new way of life.

This became the beginning of my journey in reading and education. I read with a thirst for knowledge that was the key to unlocking my true self. I read books on black history, economics, psychology, meditation – books that taught me and cultivated my greatness. I began to listen to those who shared their wisdom through their experiences. I opened my ears to the guys doing life and listened to them lament on all that they had missed out on in life. It was my education on how to be a man. I never got that growing up. I thrived in darkness for so many years of my life that when the light turned on I was all in. I am an individual that succeeds in anything I set out to do. I was living in the light and feeling its power change and transform me, revealing from within my true self, my greatness.

Reading also revealed to me that there were so many people who devoted their lives to providing the world with new knowledge, men and women whose legacy and history defined the course of our country. My world was small and my world view smaller, but when I cracked open a book my horizons widened, bringing into view ideas and knowledge that were previously unknown and counterintuitive. I felt empowered to find and define my purpose and greatness based on who I am and where I come from. I learned how to speak Swahili, and then I began to teach others how to speak it. I discovered that through teaching others, through freely passing on knowledge with no expectation of anything in return, for the sole purpose of helping another person discover their own greatness, I changed for the positive. I journeyed further into the light.

Since there is no reformation provided by the prison system, it was up to us to reform ourselves. We started a study hall where we would cut our televisions off for two hours, read a chapter out of a math book – or whatever we were reading that day – and study. Afterwards we quizzed each other through the bars on what we learned. We wrote our answers on a sheet of paper, attached it to a string tied to a bar of soap, and slid it from cell to cell correcting each other's answers.

When I was able to find like-minded people who were willing to deconstruct the negative framework built in their mind, we realized that we were the ones responsible for constructing tombs of negativity. I was not a bad person; I was just a creature looking for a better way. I conditioned myself to believe that I was an animal because that was the world I chose to live in.

I came home from prison with the mentality to do better. I kept moving forward, one foot after the other, with blinders on. I didn't look left or right to see what anyone else was doing. Within two months of being home, I was blessed with a job at Macy's in Sherman Oaks. I worked there for five years, and in that time I tried to get jobs for several of my friends. Each one failed the background check. But I, a convicted felon who just served ten years in prison, passed. These synchronicities – coincidences – are what I have come to know as God working directly in my life. He put me in that position for a reason, to be a vessel, to do His work.

After six months I was promoted to assistant dock manager, and after a year I became dock manager. I went on to work for Macy's for five years, awarded with associate of the month five times and manager of the year twice. During those five years Macy's sent me to business etiquette trainings, grammar and writing programs. They educated me about how to be a professional. They provided me the educational foundation for what I went on to do.

While I worked at Macy's, I was still active in my community. In 1999 my time came with a knock on the door. I answered and immediately recognized Bo Taylor, who was working with Hall of Fame football player Jim Brown. Bo Taylor was one of the founders who constructed gang intervention as we know it today. He asked me if I would be willing to sit down with him and other comrades from the Westside to talk about a ceasefire.

This was a big proposition with high aspirations – asking men who had been fighting and killing one another for so many years to put down their weapons and agree to peace. I was skeptical. I lived in a community that was not interested in sitting down with warring neighborhoods. Peace was not a part of the vernacular. I wanted to know what was in it for me, so I reluctantly sat down with Jim. He asked me if I was willing to take a course on the fifteen points to self-determination and mastering my own destiny. It reminded me of all the books I read in prison, all those hours spent sliding knowledge attached to soap through steel bars. In my mind it was the continuation of that. I freed my mind behind the prison bars, and this was an opportunity to chart the path for the future.

I took the course and when I completed it, Jim offered me a job as a facilitator, teaching others the same program. I let the work take me, and I took it beyond teaching in the classroom. I developed contracts with charter schools to teach the curriculum with at risk youth and young gangbangers. I traveled all over the country with other facilitators to talk with mayors, politicians, and police chiefs about gang intervention, rather than just gang suppression, telling them that suppression isn't the only option they have to deal with the problem of gang violence. I became an advocate for peace in the streets.

When Jim Brown asked me to help with a peace treaty between the warring neighborhoods on the Westside, the answer was in changing their mindset. We don't have to hang out together, and we don't have to be friends, but we also don't need to shoot each other. A lot of people did not think that would work, but in the last ten to twelve years, violence has been reduced. A lot of the credit doesn't go to us, it goes to law enforcement, but if you ask them, they will tell you that they cannot do their job without us. You can't arrest your way out of this problem. A change needs to occur in the minds on the street.

The educational part was realizing that I am not an animal, but a creature searching for a better way. When I was growing up, I didn't know any better. Negativity was the only thing I witnessed. I had five siblings raised by a single mother with no father in my life. Mom was never home. She was working two jobs trying to make sure we had the necessities of life – food, water, and shelter – so I went out into the world and it was filled with people gangbanging. The same story is played out for thousands of youth in our communities.

People say, "Wow, how'd you get out of the gang?" and my answer to them is I did not. I am still in the gang, and will be until I die. But now it is from a positive standpoint. I used to bang for a negative, now I bang for a positive. I bang for the kids, for education, for providing social services, for showing the youth how to be independent leaders and entrepreneurs in their community. I understand that gang life is a culture, and to redefine that culture, to show individuals who they are and what their greatness is, I have to be in the trenches with them. They have to see me walking the walk. It is easy to sit behind a desk, in a skyscraper downtown, high above the streets, and theorize about what urban life looks like below. But to be practitioner-based, hands on in the community, is street level. We have what is called a license to operate. I built a reputation and gained the respect of my peers through the work I put in over the years. So what

I say to them now is, "You followed me through the negative, now I am asking you to follow me through the positive." Not only am I asking you, I am leading by example. They tell their friends, "If the big homie can change, so can I." That is why I have been so successful in leading.

If I grew up in Beverly Hills or Bel-Air, I never would've been exposed to this way of life. I grew up with environmental factors that are not present in more affluent neighborhoods. My mother did her best, and she did well, but she didn't have the economic means to move us out of the hood. We live what we see and experience, and I became a product of my environment. I never would have chosen that lifestyle. I have been all the way to the top of the game in gangbanging. I've had it all and lived the gangbangers' dream with the best of them, and there is no reward. I had what I thought was the city of gold and I had nothing. The only thing at the top of this life is death and jail – a life with no purpose, a reputation that will be superseded by prison and forgotten in death.

I went through the trials of my life to get to where God wants me to be. That's what I am doing right now with community intervention. I look back on my life and I wonder, why me? Out of all the people who were running the streets at the same time I was, doing exactly what I was doing, why did I survive? There are guys who did not do half of what I did, and they are not around to talk about it. But here I am. Why becomes the obvious question. But from where I sit today I can also see the direct benefit of my community intervention work. I see firsthand the lives I have touched, the people pulled out of darkness from the brink of death, because of the work that I do. No one can do what I do the way I do it. The same is true for you. We are all here with a purpose that we are uniquely qualified to carry out.

The awareness I have now is that I am a key perfectly shaped to open the door that can save another human life. It is the most profound and gratifying feeling. We have the ability to stop the violence that has been so deeply sown and entrenched in our communities – the mothers crying, the young men and women washed away from the earth in tides of blood and drugs. It is a feeling that touches my soul.

A typical day for me involves mentoring, teaching, and coaching young men and women who are still involved in gangs and are trying to change their lives in a positive way. I understand their mindset. I've lived it. I am a product of it. Now having made it to the other side, I can extend my hand and show them how to live a meaningful life. My ideology and my focus are to change the mindset of the people I serve. Our old ideas and ways of behaving did not work. They lead us to pine boxes and steel cells. We have to change the mindset of how to live life in order to change lives. As community interventionists, we take this knowledge and blueprint for intervention and teach it around the country. People who desperately need help are provided with the tools and knowledge they need to empower themselves and their community. It is a blessing for me.

The Data

Chapter 8

Interviews with Gang Interventionists

Cris Ann Scaglione, Ph.D.

In wide-ranging monthly discussions with 20 gang interventionists in Los Angeles, their perspectives on their work, its effect on the community, their own stressors and other topics were discussed. Over a period of two years, many of these interviews were analyzed from a phenomenological perspective (Hycner, 1985), and "coded" for meaningful content (Saldaña, 2009). Coding is a process of identifying the core ideas that the people discussed and finding overarching concepts to which these ideas belonged. A few distinct but inter-related themes emerged from these conversations, which can be designated as: Relationship, Generativity, Distress, Commitment, and Work. A brief definition of these themes, and some key illustrative examples from the interviews are provided. A sixth theme, Future Needs, is discussed in another chapter.

Relationship

The most prevalent theme underlying the interviews was that of relationship. Deep, respectful, trusting relationships with members of the community, within and outside of gang culture, are at the core of everything the interventionists do. Without these relationships, the men and women doing gang intervention work would not have the trust and credibility needed to do even the simplest of tasks, such as speaking to a neighborhood kid, let alone the complex diplomacy required to get rival gangs to agree to establish a safe zone around a school, or (at the invitation of law enforcement) to help bring calm to crowds gathering

around a crime scene. The importance of relationships is found in remarks such as these:
- *It's pretty much what it is, maintaining that friendship.*
- *We all have relationships; you know what I mean? Just trying to keep that peace going.*
- *We're really deep into our community, really deep. The other day I got a phone call about some gang writing on a wall that could have led to retaliation. I talked to the kids involved, explained the situation to them, and we painted over the writing. It's the small stuff we can do to keep the community safe. I wouldn't have gotten the call if they didn't see that we are there working in the community.*
- *That's my whole thing-respect. If you want respect, you gotta give it. I always use the analogy of sports--teamwork.*
- *I represent my community, the school, the park. These are my places. We have something good and good collaborations.*
- *Effective communication and respect take you a long way.*
- *It just takes someone from inside that environment to understand.*
- *Our relationship is really big in the community. It all starts with relationship building. That is how you establish things.*

Respectful relationships between different gangs and other gang interventionists are also crucial. The interventionists spoke of the importance of being able to develop agreements between gangs within a community (e.g. between Bloods and Crips), between various factions or cliques in a gang, and between the gangs in different communities, especially between brown and black gangs (although this is much more difficult to achieve).

Intervention work between different neighborhoods is further complicated by the fact that they have different sizes, with different ethnicities and histories, and may be policed by the county sheriff's department or LAPD. The boundaries within a community may have different gangs on their borders, even on the east and west sides of the street. These challenges require various aspects of relationship skills, including a detailed knowledge of a place and its people, and the ability to maneuver between communities to form alliances and come to agreements. These arrangements may begin as temporary ceasefires, but can develop into decades-long recreational activities between different gangs.

A particularly important use of their community relationships was apparent in the gang interventionists' role in quelling community tensions during the "100 days and 100 nights." Inspired by rap lyrics, social media threatened 100 days of killing in retribution for the shooting death of a young man. There was a reported surge in gang violence, but not the eruption of homicides that was anticipated. In fact, only one gang-related homicide occurred during this crisis. This was likely due to a combination of some community policing and the mobilization of gang interventionists who, for weeks, focused on rumor control.

The ability to form sustained one-on-one relationships is also necessary for working with individuals, as when getting people out of gangs and into jobs, or genuinely connecting with kids at risk for becoming involved with a gang. Some of the current interventionists were role models, had leadership roles, and did helpful things in the community like buying groceries for homeless people, protecting kids from bullies, and coaching, even while active gang members. Some of these leadership and relationship-building skills are also part of their social toolkit when working to reduce gang violence.

Other important relationships can occur in prison. When incarcerated, rival gang members are not separated, and instead are forced to live and interact with each other. Often, as a result of these relationships, their common humanity is recognized, which can be a catalyst for growing empathy and maturation, including the decision to become a gang interventionist.

- *These dudes you locked up with are on the opposite side. They sittin' next to you when you eat. They bunkin' with you. Before you know it you become friends I started seeing the same patterns in their life and mine and realized it wasn't cool. Somethin' had to change.*

Generativity

All of the interventionists had long histories of being embedded in gangs and the larger community, and at some point, awakened to the knowledge of the damage that their lifestyle caused them, their loved ones, and the community at large. They underwent a period of profound change, often of a religious/spiritual nature, sometimes with the guidance of a mentor, and emerged with the conviction that they not only had to change their own lives, but also give back to the community. They continue to do this, not only to atone for their own actions, but also to improve the community by discouraging and preventing violence, and providing alternative activities, roles or solutions to the people (especially youth) that live there.

In a widely accepted model of development, this process is known as "generativity" (Erikson & Erikson, 1998). It usually occurs during middle age (around 40-65 years old, which is the age range of most of the interventionists) and consists of contributing something to the world that will outlast the individual, through creativity, nurturing, teaching, coaching etc. It involves taking one's accumulated life experience and giving it away to others so that they might benefit. Typical examples of this generativity include:

- *I try to use myself as an example, try to get them to use what I am giving them. We try to get these kids to understand this is a trickledown effect.*
- *It's about educating these kids, and we got to get to them at that early age, 8-14. By the time they get to junior high and high school, they should have been talked to already.*
- *I started seeing everyone I love getting murdered. Every year we was burying somebody and getting angrier and retaliating, and doing more things. I realized I needed to go out there and make things better.*
- *You look at the hurt on mother and grandmother, and you know they didn't raise you this way. You see 20, 30 years go by, and that hurricane you're in, and you're like "Whew!" It's in the eyes that you see death, and you know you can't be raising havoc anymore. At least we are here now to show people that what we were doing wasn't right, to let them know what we went through. They don't need to go through it too. At least we're planting a seed in them.*
- *My kids told me that most of their friends' fathers are dead, and some of their friends at school are dead. We made the community the way it is, and we have to atone for it. I know I do, if I want to take that burden, that karma, off my children. I gotta do something about it.*
- *I just want to continue to be that vessel for help. My thing is to make a negative into a positive, to show people that they can do good, do better than what I did and what my generation did.*

Distress

The lives of all the gang interventionists are peppered with losses and traumas. All have witnessed and otherwise experienced numerous deaths of people they knew and often loved. Most had brushes with their own death, often by being shot or stabbed--sometimes on more than one occasion. In some ways their pain is even greater after their decision to become gang interventionists, as they have become more emotionally vulnerable, empathetic, and keenly aware of the cost of violence, especially across generations.

All of the interventionists reported deep grief and key losses that pain them deeply. Some of these events occurred years in the past, and many were ongoing. All of them mentioned at least one key death that motivated them to become interventionists and spurred them to continue. More recent losses that are keenly felt are of particularly tragic deaths. Most of the interventionists told stories like these:

- *It was this young lady we'd been working with for a while. She was out of the gang life and started working. She had a boyfriend, went back to school and she loved her little job. She was pregnant and was going to a movie with her boyfriend. She wasn't gone 10 minutes when a gang pulled up with some AKs shooting at someone else, and they killed her and her baby and her boyfriend. She, the memory of her, just sits with me today. She had her whole life ahead of her. She was changing, and they were going to be on their way.*
- *She just graduated from high school and went out to celebrate. Their party was cancelled, so she went to one in a different neighborhood. I told her not to go, but she went with her friends anyway. An hour later I got the call. She had been shot. That devastated her mama. To this day you can't see her mama without feeling sorry for her. She still cries and says she*

- *missed her baby, and you know there's nothing you can do. She was so happy, then ended up just dead.*
- *It really hurts because you make a connection with these kids, and you hear that something happened to them, and you say, "No, he was just right here." We just did safe passage with him yesterday. You wake up and they're gone. You can be mad. You can be upset, but what are you going to do? It's just sad.*
- *I been in them hospital rooms when their mama finds out they're dead. There is that cry that comes from them that's indescribable. It's like part of life is leaving them. Even when they leave, you still hear that sound.*
- *We understand where each of us came from. We're tired and realize too, that you been burying kids. That's the worst thing in the world.*

The work of a gang interventionist is, in and of itself, stress-inducing. They have lengthy, unpredictable schedules and are often available 24/7. They are continuously exposed to ongoing traumatic situations, and work towards high-stakes goals, often under pressure, and with few resources. Not surprisingly, many interventionists reported that they get very little sleep. Distressing nighttime phone calls are common, containing bad news, emergency notifications or calls from distraught family members. (e.g. *She called me yesterday, and gave me the chills, but she can't talk to nobody but me. She doesn't want to live anymore.*)

Gang intervention programs are often understaffed and underfunded, and the workers are overloaded. Many receive death threats, sometimes from members of their own or other gangs, either due to some past conflict, or because of the work they currently do. One group reported losing two of their team members over a short time, due to gang violence. Both were killed while on their way home from

their work as interventionists. Many mentioned their stress and trauma openly (though usually briefly):
- *I realized I have a lot of trauma that I carry with me.*
- *I broke down crying in that training because I realized I've been carrying this trauma since I was a kid. I see the trauma that all these other people are carrying, and you realize you're not equipped to help them get over it.*
- *Doing this work isn't easy.*
- *It could be real stressful, very stressful.*
- *I have just been weeping so much. So much killing. It's hit home. It has been a lot of funerals. Like every week. We took some big losses for a couple of months.*
- *I am stressing. They're stressing. Their mom is stressing. Don't think we don't get tired.*
- *If you do gang work for so long, it will impact you negatively if you're not careful.*

While most interventionists enjoy cooperative and respectful interactions with law enforcement, several interventionists noted that they are disrespected and harassed by police. Despite being known in the community for their gang intervention work, some are pulled over without cause, others are called "old gangstas" by officers, and some reported that their activities are aggressively "monitored," including being encircled by police on motorcycles or horses, during daytime public park activities such as a baseball game or barbecue. Besides adding stress to their lives, this level of uncooperativeness limits the effectiveness of their work.

In a dissertation by Raichel (2018), 14 of the same gang interventionists interviewed for this project participated in additional interviews and testing of their perceived levels of stress. Not surprisingly, the gang interventionists were found to have moderate to high levels of perceived stress. Hoping that this stress might decrease with time on the job, stress levels were compared across years of experience ("intermediate": 5.0-9.9 years, "professional": 10-14.9 years and "expert": 15 + years). Unsurprisingly, given the difficulty of this work, their perceived stress did not lessen over time.

Commitment

Because of their ongoing stress and trauma, and difficult, exhausting work, many of the interventionists admitted that they sometimes feel like giving up. However, no one expressed being hopeless, and they keep going because they know their work is necessary. They feel that they have a calling, and they are committed to seeing it through. (e.g. *I am called to do this. This is God calling. It ain't nobody else. I am still here for a reason, and that is to try to make things better.*) Many reported doing their work without funding for long periods, sometimes for years (one reported running a neighborhood program for 8 years without funding).

Some reported that their commitment is occasionally reinforced when they see they're getting through to people (especially youth), or when they encounter someone they haven't seen in years who thanks them for what they did for them. Their efforts to help prevent harm and create safety (especially for kids) sometimes have visible effects, and the interventionists know they're making a difference:

- *You're constantly talking, and sometimes you want to throw your hands up, but you find that one kid, and you know that you can do something different for them.*
- *You're thinking you've done all this for nothing, then you see someone coming around the corner, and they ask if you remember them, and you talk and you find out they doing well. It gets you to your reward, and*

you realize it's worth it, and you aren't wasting your time.
- *I feel this is where I should be, where God wanted me. It ain't easy, but at the end of the day it is rewarding when you see the kid getting their diploma, or you learn they moved on and got a job.*

Work

The actual day-to-day tasks that the gang interventionists engage in are numerous. Some are formally indexed in monthly reports, but many are not. The interventionists spoke with pride of their work, and although their tasks are discussed in other chapters, they will be mentioned briefly here as well, since it was a major portion of what they spontaneously discussed in their interviews. The activities also illustrate the practical application of the previously mentioned themes (especially relationship and commitment). The main types of activities discussed were:

1. Establishing safe passage/safe zones: routes where kids can walk to and from school, sometimes crossing different gang territories without being attacked or approached by gangs in the area. When a formal safe passage agreement is not in place, interventionists will often personally escort kids to and from school.
2. Gang engagement: direct conversation and negotiation between leaders and members of rival gangs to accomplish a common goal, such as the establishment of a safe passage zone.
3. Peace agreements: involve reaching a cease-fire agreement, but may evolve into activities such as inviting two rival gangs to come to a public park for a shared activity, like a game of baseball or football. In one instance, this agreement has held for about 20 years.

4. Rumor control: in-person or online dispelling rumors and disseminating verified facts. This requires the respect and credibility earned through community relationships and acting with integrity.
5. Crowd control: defusing crowd tensions, usually after a shooting. Often involves rumor control as well.
6. Family interventions: working with distraught family members after a shooting or other crime. This often goes with crowd control, and includes long-term accessibility and follow-up with families (much of which is informal/unreported).
7. Girls and Gangs: educational groups for girls involved with, or at risk of involvement with gangs. Includes life skills training, rumor control, and possibly providing additional services for transportation, homelessness, job search, post-incarceration advising, mentoring, gang intervention etc.
8. School programs: these run the gamut from formal educational and safe zone interventions to informal on-call activities. Sometimes the requests are inappropriate, such as calling a gang interventionist because a kid brought a gun to school, instead of contacting the armed, contracted school security staff. In order to reduce possibility of violent encounter with armed security, the interventionist might choose to intervene.
9. Parks after Dark: sports leagues, tutoring, life skills training, arts and crafts and other supervised, structured after-school activities in public parks.
10. Formal gang intervention programs, such as VIDA (Vital Intervention and Directional Alternatives), ABLA (A Better LA), and GRP (Gang Reduction Program).

11. Various community supported activities (some with coordinated police involvement). Though not recorded in monthly logs, gang interventionists are often present at various community-based activities, such as:
    - the Peace Walk--a 24-hour walk promoting peace in urban neighborhoods
    - events with food giveaways, free medical services and raffles for home appliances
    - Mothers of Incarcerated Children providing transportation, care packages, court support and other services for mothers whose children are in jail
    - other park activities, including an annual memorial for those who died as a result of gang violence
    - RBI (Reviving Baseball in Inner Cities) program with the LA Dodgers.

In addition to these formal programs, most of the gang interventionists are also available all day, every day for phone calls. Many of these are from grieving parents and other loved ones. Other calls are tips from neighbors about things going on that might spell trouble, to which the interventionist will respond in order to head off escalating tensions or open conflict. Many also coach teams and do community education outside of formal gang intervention programs.

The growth and awakening that these men and women experience creates not just the desire to atone and to help, but the ongoing commitment to consistently show up to work for change (generativity and commitment). They use their connections with the community to build respect and credibility and forge new connections across gang, neighborhood and community boundaries (relationship). They are able to effect incremental changes, provide emotional and material support, and often prevent acts of violence through their daily work. This exacts a continuing physical and emotional toll (distress), yet they continue to grow and remain hopeful and resilient. As one gang interventionist put it, "When you do this work, you grow into a person."

Chapter 9

Looking to the Future

Cris Ann Scaglione, Ph.D.

There is much room for improved, informed services to reduce violence and gang activity, especially in the largely underserved lower income urban communities of Los Angeles. The future of gang intervention and related research entails many moving parts, some of which will be mentioned here, based largely on the discussions with gang interventionists.

Future Needs

Based on their experience, the gang interventionists interviewed for this project had many perspectives, from the local to the international, regarding the factors that cause and maintain the conditions that produce criminal gangs. They had concrete suggestions for things that would make their work more effective. (This is the "Future Needs" theme mentioned in a previous chapter about these interviews).

Resources and structure

Nearly everyone mentioned the need for more people doing gang intervention, as well as consistent funding, planning/policy, and training. The experience of "hit and miss" funding, as one interventionist noted, creates chaos, rifts within the community, and contributes to a "poverty mindset." Policy suggestions included providing further education for teachers and principals regarding rumor contagion especially in an age of social media. Others recommended a comprehensive structure in schools for working with kids at risk of gang violence or involvement. Frequent discussion of the need for ongoing training for gang interventionists was necessary, and some observed that some interventionists were "not as skilled," especially for dealing with "hot" or complex problems.

Several gang interventionists also recommended additional continuing education of police regarding their procedures and protocols, especially regarding the use of an aggressive tone and body language, such as keeping their hands on their weapons. They also suggested a change to community policing (allocating police officers to particular areas so that they become familiar with the people and issues of the neighborhood).

Collaborative networks

Many gang interventionists discussed greater coordination between jurisdictions (especially county vs. city), as well as the need for accessible communication networks between agencies, and other interventionists. One example of the importance of enhanced capacity to communicate with each other occurred when a man died of a drug overdose. Almost immediately, social media messages circulated that he had been killed by a rival gang. Neighborhood gang interventionists had to investigate this on their own, clarified and verified the actual situation, and then had to go to "gang hot spots" to dispel rumors and disseminate the truth. This would have been much quicker and easier if a communication network had been available.

In a related theme, the role of social media was frequently discussed, related to the instigation of more tension and violence through bullying and especially the uncontrolled spread of rumors. Countering the effects of Instagram (dubbed "Murdergram" in popular culture) and other social media is made more difficult by the use of false identities, and the presence of agitators from outside of the community, or even out-of-state. This is a large, loosely-linked collaborative network that gang interventionists must work against. Some interventionists have suggested that they

need a larger community presence to counter the effects of social media. Some relevant remarks include:
- *(commenting on the effects of social media) They write here and there, then it can explode, and we have a whole community fight.*
- *There are the "sneaky ones" with false names, and people out of state agitating for violence.*
- *(commenting on graphic posting of man dying after being shot) People don't have common sense, and that emotional part seems to be gone; they just post.*

Problems of the community at large

Many gang interventionists suggested the need to deal with entrenched problems in the community, and were aware of the contributions of social, political, economic and government policies affecting them, especially since the 1960's. They often remarked on the increased disparity of wealth, the disappearance of the middle class from the neighborhoods, and an influx of increasingly poor and/or culturally different members of society, including immigrants. Many observed that their community had become much less coherent and stable, and regretted the breakdown of the family and loss of "community parenting" (adults keeping an eye on the activities and whereabouts of all of the kids in the neighborhood and intervening if needed).

Much discussion also focused on the mental health costs of worsening societal conditions, and the need to reduce addiction, fear and trauma in the community, since those factors contribute to a multigenerational cycle of trauma and violence. Drug addiction and "crack babies" were mentioned several times in the context of unmindful, impulsive and violent behavior because they "*don't know better.*" Typical comments regarding trauma included:
- *That's what's wrong with these kids--so much trauma that's sitting inside bubbling. They've been seeing*

> *this shooting, stabbing and fighting. So you figure they went to sleep with a nightmare, then they get up and go back outside and see the areas where that person was laid, and they go to school where it is talked about among their friends, and not the right person.*

- *It's this trauma that keeps a lot of what's going on in the streets still-unresolved trauma.*
- *When Daddy has a gun on the table, or Mommy's boyfriend comes in with a gun, that's all they know.*
- *If you don't know how to channel that anger or release it, it becomes more death. Unfortunately, that hate is deeply embedded.*
- *The kids have multigenerational PTSD, especially from seeing family members get killed, and the victims of trauma become perpetrators of trauma.*

Multigenerational dysfunction and trauma were also understood to put kids at risk due to poor/absent parenting, so children had too much responsibility (running the household), and/or had too much freedom.

Brown vs. black gang culture

Some especially cogent discussions about how to improve things in the future was based on the need to understand the differences between black and brown culture and their gangs. Latino gangs currently function more like organized crime within national and international networks. They were described as focused on the larger organization and not just "street work." In turn, the larger organizations were painted as being more widely distributed, regimented, multigenerational and collectivist-minded than African-American gangs. Some gang interventionists also mentioned that although there are "cliques" in all gangs, some Latino gangs have dozens of cliques and a "*super-predator vibe.*"

Regrettably, the training model for gang intervention is a "black" model that is not always relevant or useful for

Latinos. Not adhering to the model also affects the funding of gang intervention activities and programs in large areas such as Watts and south central regions of Los Angeles that now have a majority Latino population. There is ongoing black-brown gang tension in these regions, which is severe enough to have been characterized as a race war since about 1997. (This is well documented in news media and gang documentaries.) Gang interventionists emphasize the need to work collaboratively with Latino gangs, but this is tricky without a clear model or approach for people to use in a complex, international organization. Many said the biggest challenge was trying not to violate the numerous boundaries within the gangs and their various factions and levels of organization.

Future Research and Intervention

Gang intervention efforts are about as old as gangs themselves, but the study of details of their experience, and the effectiveness of their interventions is rare (in part because it can hinder interventionists' ability to function and even endanger their lives). Since this is a new area of study, continued phenomenological work will remain the method of choice (studying the subjective experience of the interventionists). In addition, including quantitative measures (tests) of the types of factors mentioned by the gang interventionists, such as stress, trauma, and commitment to their work, might easily be included. Whenever possible, qualitative (perspectives and experiences), and quantitative (tests of stress, etc.) information from community members affected by the work of gang interventionists should also be gathered.

The interventionists themselves made excellent suggestions for further study into areas of social justice and socio-economic improvement, the multigenerational spread of trauma and violence, and similar broad-reaching topics that, if better understood, might improve community functioning, and contribute to better public policy and training for schools, police and gang interventionists. One particularly useful area to quickly delve into is ethnic and other cultural differences, especially between Latino and African-American gangs and culture. In consultation with Latino gang interventionists, this research could lead to more culturally appropriate and effective intervention strategies for Latino gangs. Presumably, similar research could be conducted with the Asian, Pacific Islander, white and mixed-ethnicity gangs in LA County.

Understanding generational differences in gang culture and the community at large is also important. The role of social media was often discussed in the context of provoking violence. However, it might also be useful for gang interventionists to utilize social media more extensively themselves, not just to dampen rhetoric and control rumors, but to add to their community profile. Younger, more techy-savvy members of the community can help promote the activities, services and ethos of the gang interventionists. This can be done across many platforms and could raise the social profile of gang intervention activities. The use of social media may also make it easier to develop the communication networks that many interventionists wanted to be enhanced.

One of the most difficult challenges for future research involves formal efficacy studies. When complex multidimensional subjects such as gang or community violence are examined, it is very difficult to pinpoint a single factor that might be causing changes in behavior and levels of violence. Broad indices like crime statistics cannot reflect a 1:1 correspondence between gang intervention and crime rates, no matter how meaningful or impactful those interventions may have been. Crime statistics may not even be sensitive to police activities, or even represent the actual types and rates of criminal activity in a region, but instead may reflect large scale socioeconomic changes in a community.

The gang interventionists provided anecdotal evidence of some of their successes, including:
- Many deaths were probably prevented by establishment of safe passage and 1:1 escorts with gang interventionists.
- After a program started in one particular neighborhood, most kids had jobs, or joined the military, and some moved out of state instead of getting involved in gang life.
- A 10-20 year peace agreement (families from rival gangs meeting at park to play baseball, football, and have the kids play together).

Several also speculated about who gets credit when things go well (e.g. *How do we get credit for the work? If we have a gang shooting, and nobody retaliates, who gets credit?*). This comment also brings up an important point about research--it is biased towards counting and tracking events, not non-events. This shortcoming can be overcome, but requires speculation based on previous estimates of the probability of certain events, based on past conditions. Much like predicting the weather this can be difficult, especially if current conditions are new or unique (and presuming there is enough information gathered over a long enough period of time to have a good baseline index of previous circumstances).

As interesting and potentially useful as accounts of clearly successful interventions may be, they are not sufficient to prove that gang interventions effectively reduce gang related violence and crime. The scaling or size of efficacy research usually has to be over long periods of time, and on both a very small and very large scale. On a small scale, phenomenological studies such as personal accounts and case studies can provide some proof of effectiveness.

The use of "psychological autopsy" work sometimes done after a suicide (Isometsä, 2001) might be useful, but would have to take broader social/environmental context into consideration.

On a larger scale, we would have to examine gang violence trends over long periods of time, especially in comparison to similar circumstances with little to no gang intervention (an unlikely event) and take into consideration large socioeconomic and possibly geopolitical conditions. As daunting as this is, it is a worthy enterprise to engage in. It will take a long time, similar to other efficacy and outcome research of areas like family dysfunction, experiences of childhood trauma, or even smoking. This study represents a small step towards understanding the nature and effectiveness of gang interventions, and we are grateful for the generous participation of the interventionists.

Chapter 10

Summary

How do you summarize violence intervention work? How do you end work that you began more than a decade ago? How do you reflect on memories that lead you on your path of becoming who you are? How do you say this is the end to hugs, tears and support?
You don't!
This work will not end. You read the literature, the stories and data. This work cannot end. It will not end. It is as necessary to the communities it serves as nourishment is to the human body. The work continues every day, every minute, by the work these brave men and women do, by the small interactions that take place in the community, by all the lives touched by this work. Right now as you are reading this, the work is continuing. You have been exposed. This is where your path has started being altered even if you don't know it because of the knowledge that has been gained by reading this book. So now that you know, I ask this question:
What will you do with this knowledge?
Next question:
How will you affect those around you?
You don't have to take on the task or work presented here, but you can do what is within your ability to do. It could be that when you are interacting in the world, you pause before you judge someone because that person could be an interventionist serving their community and you. I am sure by now you have looked at the pictures on the back of this book. You likely had an impression when you first saw them. But if you have taken the time to read this book, your impression is likely different now. By even picking up this book, you began the process of change. I urge you to hold

that thought and hold yourself accountable for how you can be a change agent.

About the Authors

Michael Oropollo, Jr.

Michael Oropollo is a bestselling author and teacher. His social and political essays have been published in the Santa Monica Daily Press and the Good Men Project, where he was a weekly columnist. He is the author of *Thoughts*, a poetry volume, *Beyond the Bars: From the Prison to the Podium* with Chris "Tatted Strength" Luera, and *His History, Her Story* with Dr. Warner.

Debra Warner, Psy.D.

Dr. Debra Warner received her Master of Arts and Master of Education in counseling psychology from Columbia University, Teachers College, in New York City. She completed her doctorate in Forensic Psychology from Alliant International University in Fresno, California. She has served as an adjunct professor for several universities and as lead faculty for Chapman University's Marriage and Family Therapy program. She is currently a full professor in The Chicago School of Professional Psychology's Psy.D. program in Clinical Forensic Psychology in Los Angeles. She has also served as Special Assistant to the Dean of Academic Affairs: Diversity and Community Engagement and Lead Faculty for the Forensic Psychology department for The Chicago School of Professional Psychology in both Los Angeles and Irvine. Her previous professional assignments include: U.S. Department of Homeland Security, Los Angeles Police Department, C.U.R.E., A Better LA, U.S. Department of Defense, California Department of Corrections & Rehabilitation and Regional Center. For these assignments, she designed program elements related to community gang intervention, mental health and evaluation. She has also served as clinical supervisor relating to human trafficking, trauma, PTSD and multicultural therapeutic techniques.

Currently, her research focuses on diversity issues connected to forensic community mental health and male survivor trauma. She has focused her career on assisting survivors with emotional issues related to trauma violence and abuse. In 2008 she was asked to create an anti-recidivism program for the Los Angeles Police Department focusing on environmental needs that stem from problematic environments. In 2014 she assisted with a creating mental health curriculum for a community gang intervention program, the Professional Community Intervention Training Institute (PCITI). She is an advisory board member of A Better LA, a nonprofit that works in community gang intervention. She is also a frequent speaker pertaining to community gang intervention and has assisted with talks that were presented at the United Nations' Safer Cities Conference. In 2015 she founded, together with PCITI, the Summit on Community Resilience, Intervention, Prevention, and Training (SCRIPT), an annual conference on male trauma, violence and abuse with a focus on community interactions from all backgrounds.

In 2009 she received several awards and recognitions for community engagement from the Los Angeles City Attorney, U.S. Department of Defense, Los Angeles Police Department and The Chicago School of Professional Psychology. In 2013 she was given a distinguished teaching award for Outstanding Public Service Teaching. She currently is a peer reviewer on several academic journals and is part of the Medical Advisory Board for Quality Health. In 2015 she became a regular Tuesday night co-host of the weekly syndicated radio show *Stop Child Abuse Now* (SCAN) on Blog Talk Radio with Bill Murray. She served on the board of directors for The National Partnership to End Interpersonal Violence Across the Lifespan (NPEIV) relating to public awareness and publicity. She has written a number of encyclopedia entries related to crime and justice for Sage publications (*Encyclopedia of Transnational Crime and Justice* and *Encyclopedia of Criminal Justice Ethics*). Her book about male survivor relationships with significant others, *His History, Her Story* was released in October 2017. In her spare time, she creates training programs for law enforcement and attorneys related to mental health and the court system. It should be noted that in all of her professional endeavors, she involves students for their professional development.

References

Chapter 1

Alonso, A. A. (2004). Racialized identities and the formation of Black gangs in Los Angeles. *Urban Geography, 25*(7), 658-674.

Coughlin, B. C., & Venkatesh, S. A. (2003). The urban street gang after 1970. *Annual Review of Sociology, 29*(1), 41-64.

Decker, S. H., Van Gemert, F., & Pyrooz, D. C. (2009). Gangs, migration, and crime: The changing landscape in Europe and the USA. *Journal of International Migration and Integration/Revue de l'integration et de la migration internationale, 10*(4), 393-408.

Federal Bureau of Investigation (January 7, 2016). Transnational gangs: Part 1: Understanding the threat. Retrieved from https://www.fbi.gov/news/stories/transnational-gangs.

Hagedorn, J. M. (1998). Gang violence in the postindustrial era. *Crime and Justice, 24*, 365-419.

Hagedorn, J. M. (2005). The global impact of gangs. *Journal of Contemporary Criminal Justice, 21*(2), 153-169.

Hagedorn, J. M. (2006). Race not space: A revisionist history of gangs in Chicago. *The Journal of African American History, 91*(2), 194-208.

Howell, J. C. & Griffiths, E. A. (2015). *Gangs in America's Communities* (2nd ed.). Thousand Oaks: SAGE Publishing.

Howell, J. C., & Moore, J. P. (2010). History of street gangs in the United States. [Bulletin]. Washington, D.C.: US Department of Justice.

McLean, R., Robinson, G., & Densley, J. (2018). The rise of drug dealing in the life of the North American street gang. *Societies, 8*(3), 90.

People v. Zamora, 1942 66 Cal. App.2d, 174.

Pyrooz, D., Decker, S., & Fleisher, M. (2011). From the street to the prison, from the prison to the street: Understanding and responding to prison gangs. *Journal of Aggression, Conflict and Peace Research, 3*(1), 12-24.

Sante, L. (1991). *Low Life: Lures and Snares of Old New York.* New York: Vintage Books.

Simon, T. R., Ritter, N. M., & Mahendra, R. R. (2013). Changing course: Preventing gang membership.

Telles, E. M., & Ortiz, V. (2008). *Generations of exclusion: Mexican-Americans, assimilation, and race.* Russell Sage Foundation.

Vigil, J. D. (2003). Urban violence and street gangs. *Annual Review of Anthropology, 32*(1), 225-242.

Zhou, M., & Lee, R. (2015). Traversing ancestral and new homelands: Chinese immigrant transnational organizations in the United States. *The state and the grassroots: Immigrant transnational organizations in four continents,* 27-50.

Chapter 2

A Better LA (2016). Funded Programs. Retrieved April 26, 2018, from http://www.abetterla.org/programs/

Best Practices to Address Community Gang Problems. (2010). DoJ Office of Juvenile Justice and Delinquency Prevention. Retrieved from https://www.ncjrs.gov/pdffiles1/ojjdp/231200.pdf

Cardenas, T. (2008). "A Guide for Understanding Effective Community-Based Gang Intervention, Volume II." City of Los Angeles.

Crime Mapping and COMPSTAT. (2010). Retrieved from

http://www.lapdonline.org/crime_mapping_and_compstat

Dunworth, T., Hayeslip, D., Lyons, M., & Denver, M. (2010). Evaluation of the Los Angeles Gang Reduction and Youth Development Program: Final Y1 Report. Retrieved from http://www.urban.org/uploadedpdf/412251-LAGang-Reduction.pdf

Gang Reduction and Youth Development Newton GRYD Needs Assessment Final Report. (2010). City of Los Angeles, Advancement Project. Retrieved from http://mayor.lacity.org/stellent/groups/electedofficials/

Gang Reduction and Youth Development Watts/Southeast GRYD Needs Assessment Final Report. (2010). City of Los Angeles, Advancement Project. Retrieved from http://www.ci.la.ca.us/mayor/stellent/groups/electedofficials/@myr_ch_contributor/documents/contributor_web_content/lacity_004912.pdf

Guilfoyle, J.J. (n.d.). Gang prevention programs in greater Los Angeles. Retrieved from https://priceschool.usc.edu/students/review-journal/policy-and-practice-2012-2013/gang-prevention-programs-in-greater-los-angeles/

H.E.L.P.E.R. Foundation (2012). Gang Intervention Chart. Retrieved April 26, 2018, from http://helperfoundation.org/gangintervention.html

P.C.I. People for Community Improvement. (n.d.). In *Facebook* [Page type]. Retrieved from https://www.facebook.com/pcicenter13008/

R.A.C.E. (n.d.). R.A.C.E. Retrieved from http://race4communities.org/home.html

Rice, C. (2007). A Call to Action: A Case for a Comprehensive Solution to L.A.'s Gang Violence Epidemic. Los Angeles: Advancement Project.

Serjeant, J. (2007). Little glamour in L.A., "Gang Capital of America". Retrieved from http://www.reuters.com/article/2007/02/09/us-gangs-losangelesculture-idUSN0846153020070209

Summer Night Lights Program Overview. (2011). City of Los Angeles. Retrieved from http://mayor.lacity.org/Issues/GangReduction/SummerNightLights/index.htm

The Professional Community Intervention Institute. (n.d.). Impact. Retrieved from http://www.pciti.net/impact.html

Toberman Neighborhood Center. (2014). Gang prevention & intervention. Retrieved from http://www.toberman.org/programs/gang-intervention

Chapter 8

Erikson, E. H. & Erikson J. M. (1998). *Life cycle completed.* New York, NY: W. W. Norton.

Hycner, R. H. (1985). Some guidelines for the phenomenological analysis of interview data. *Human Studies 8*, 279-303.

Raichel C. D. (2018) *Stress on the streets: Measuring perceived stress of active gang interventionists* (Unpublished doctoral dissertation). The Chicago School of Professional Psychology, Los Angeles.

Saldaña, J. (2009). *The coding manual for researchers.* Thousand Oaks, CA: Sage.

Chapter 9
Isometsä E. T. (2001). Psychological autopsy studies--a review. *European Psychiatry, 16(7)*:379-85

CPSIA information can be obtained
at www.ICGtesting.com
Printed in the USA
FSHW011919070719
59737FS